THIS BOOK BELONG TO

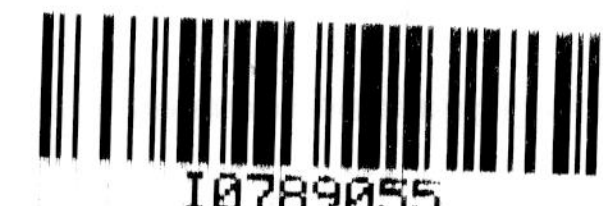

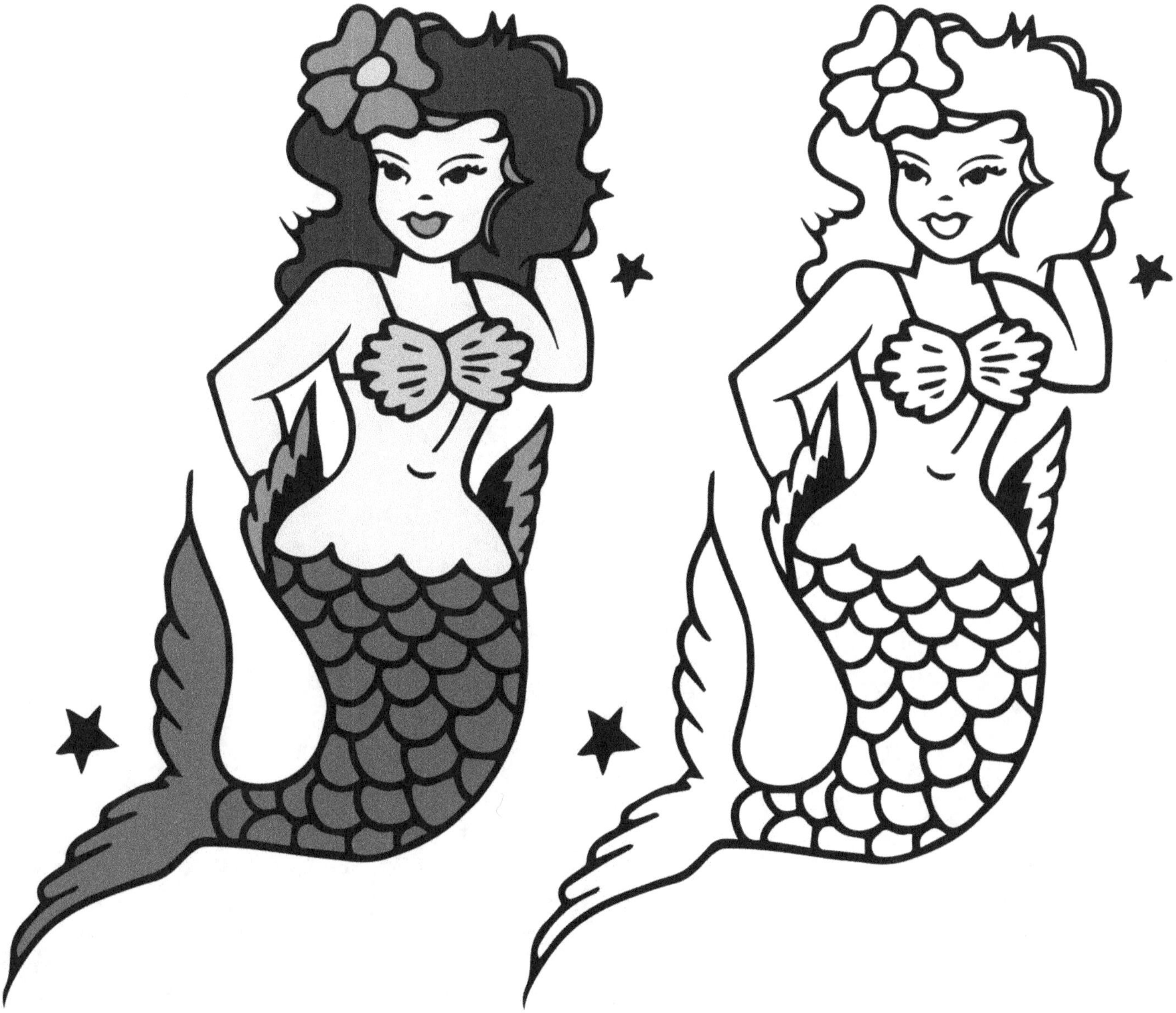

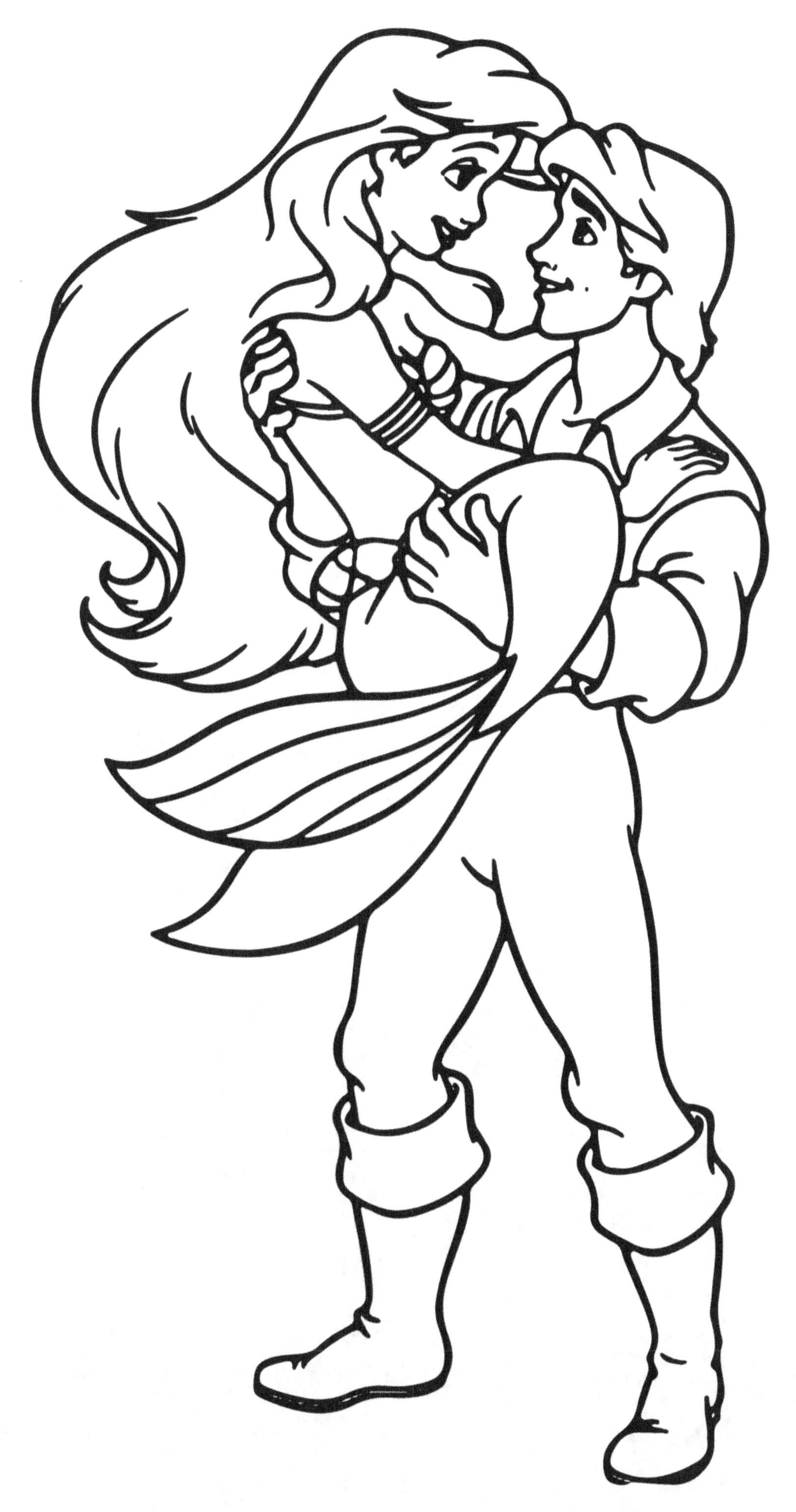

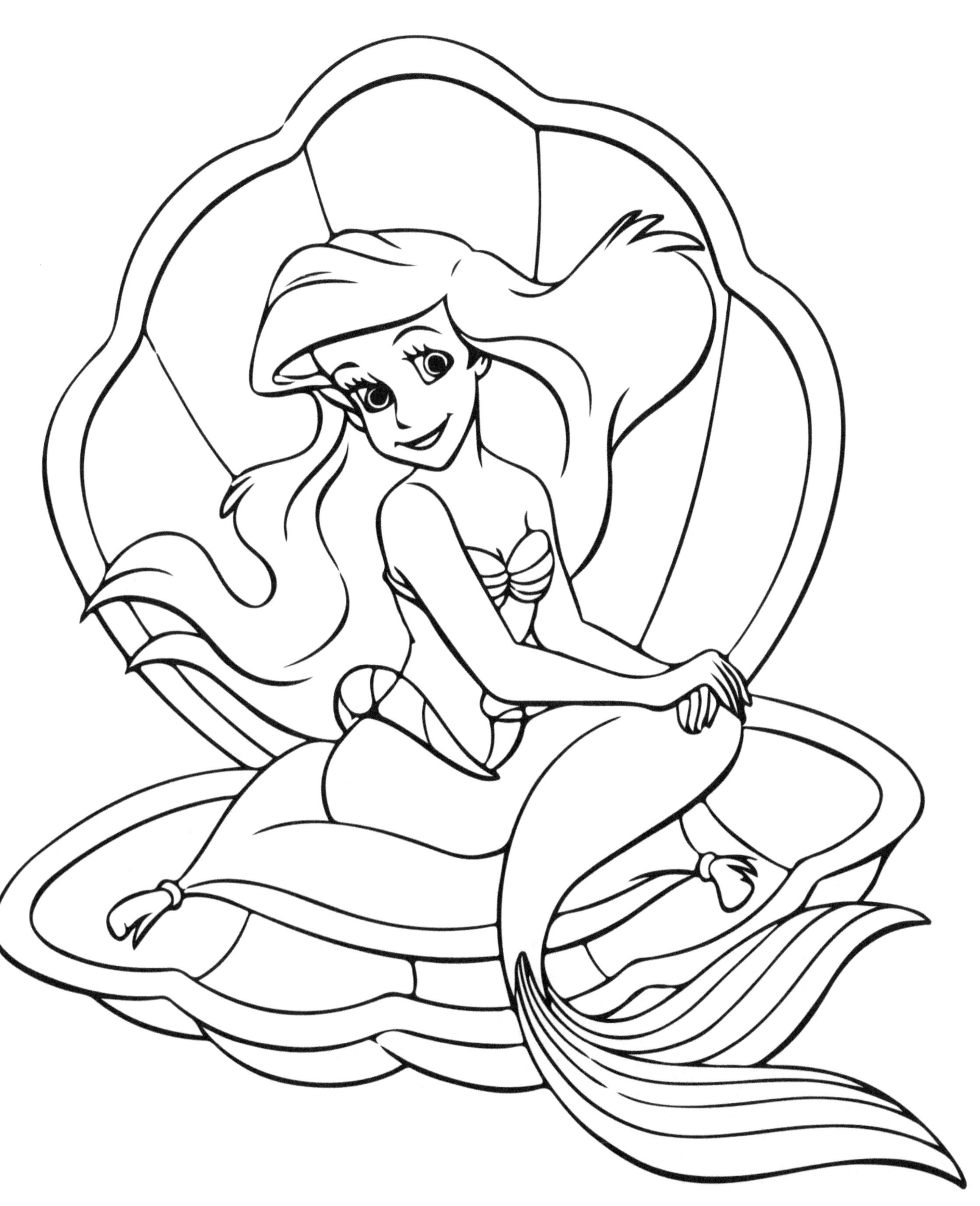

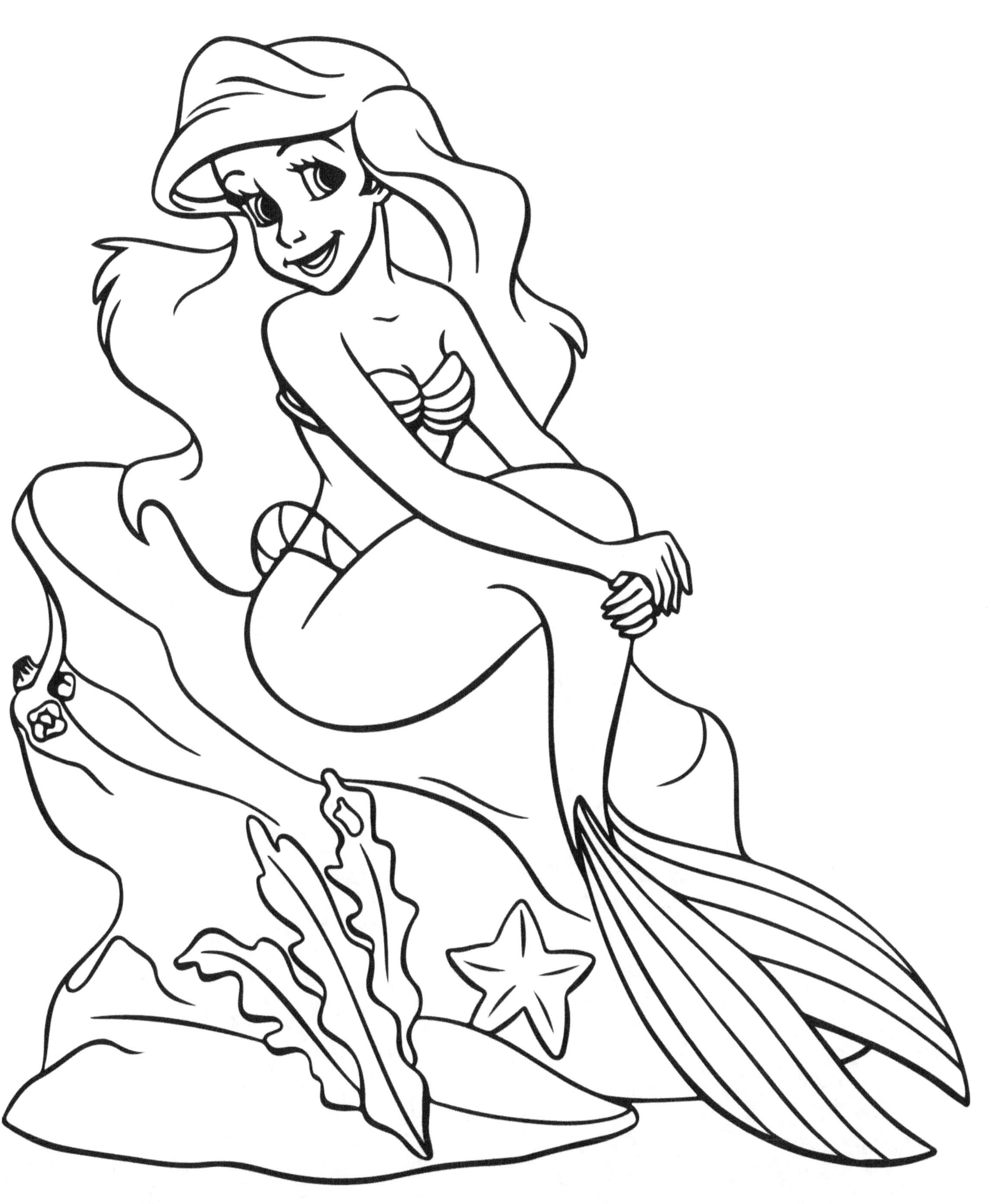

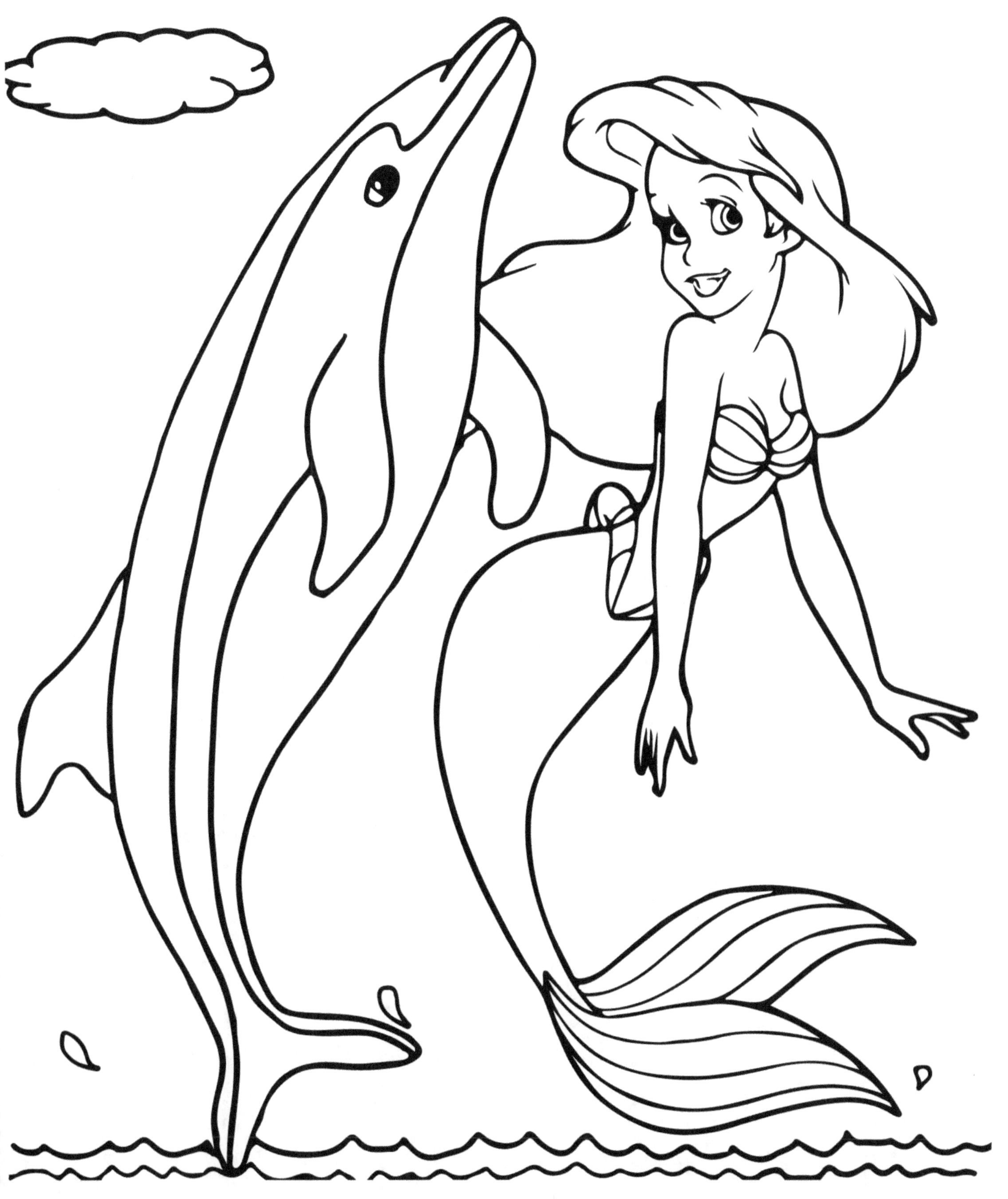

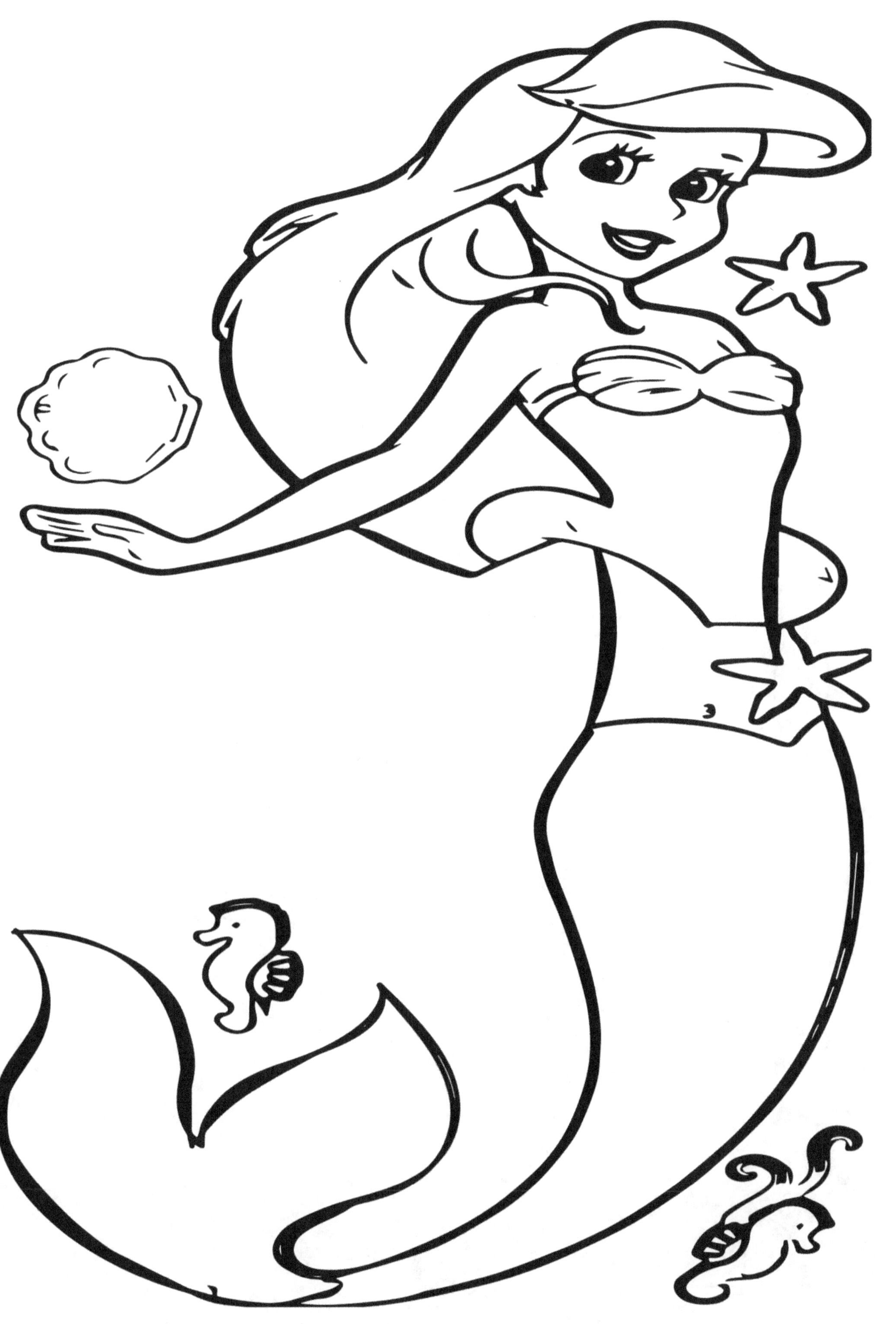

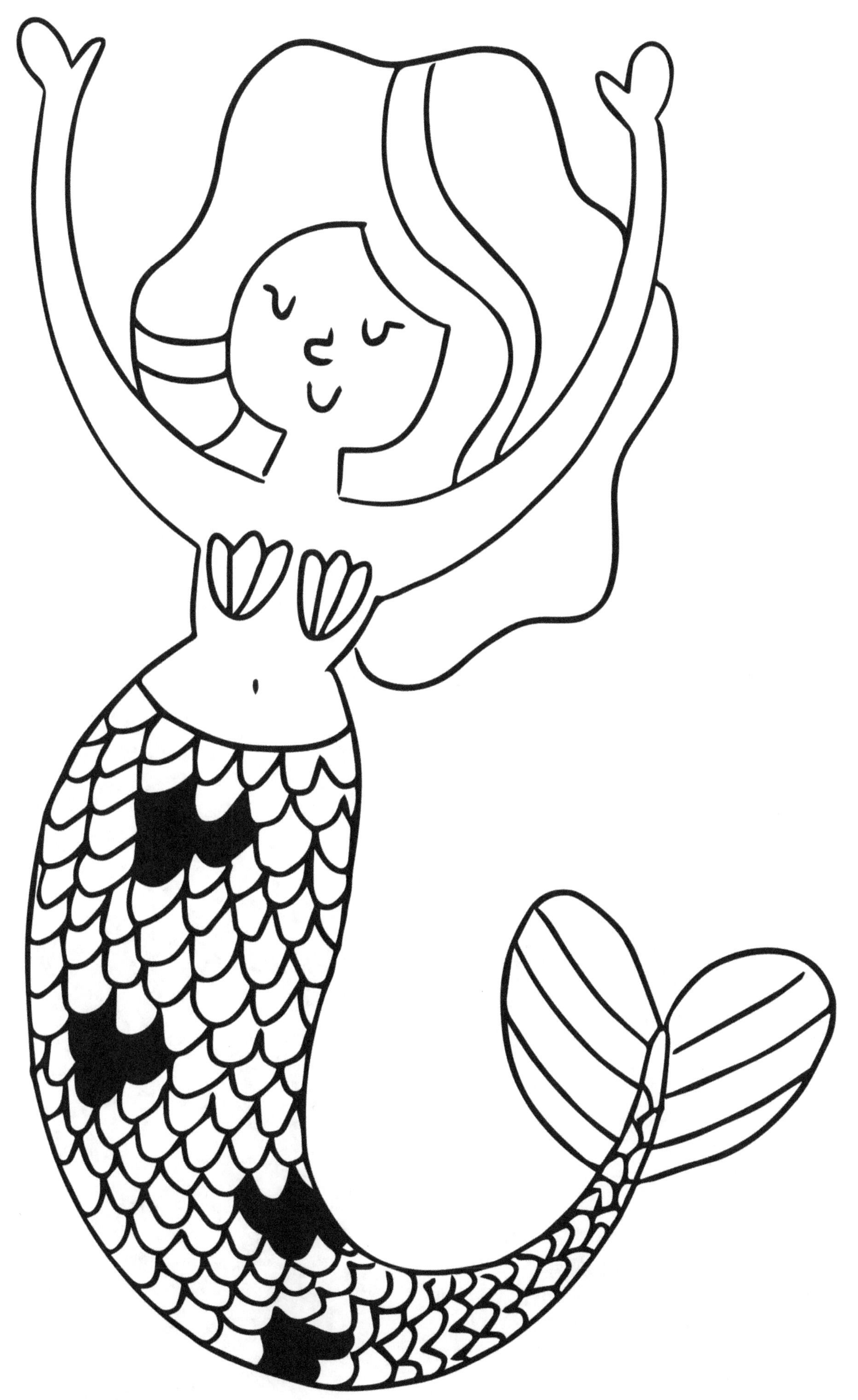

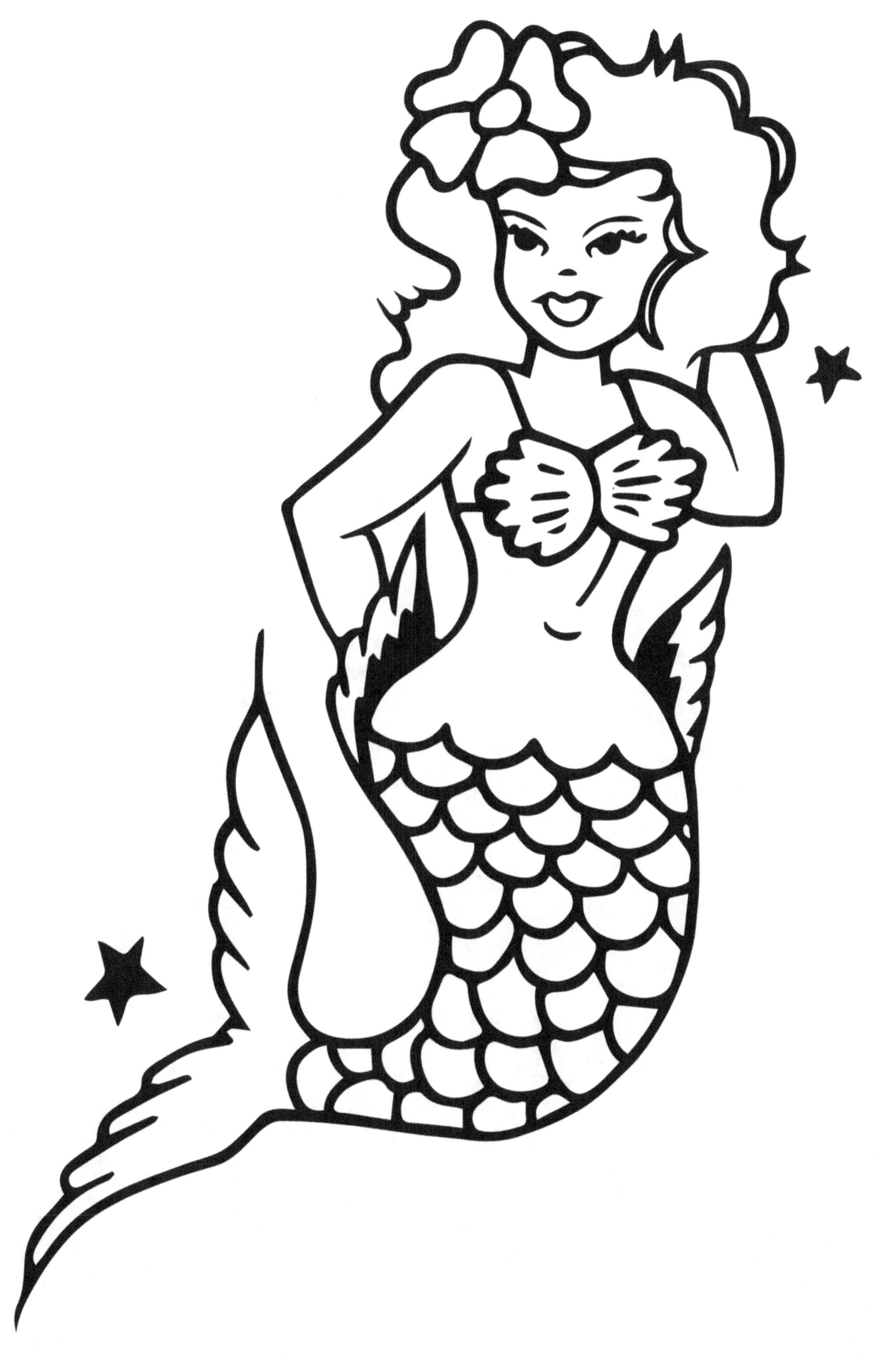

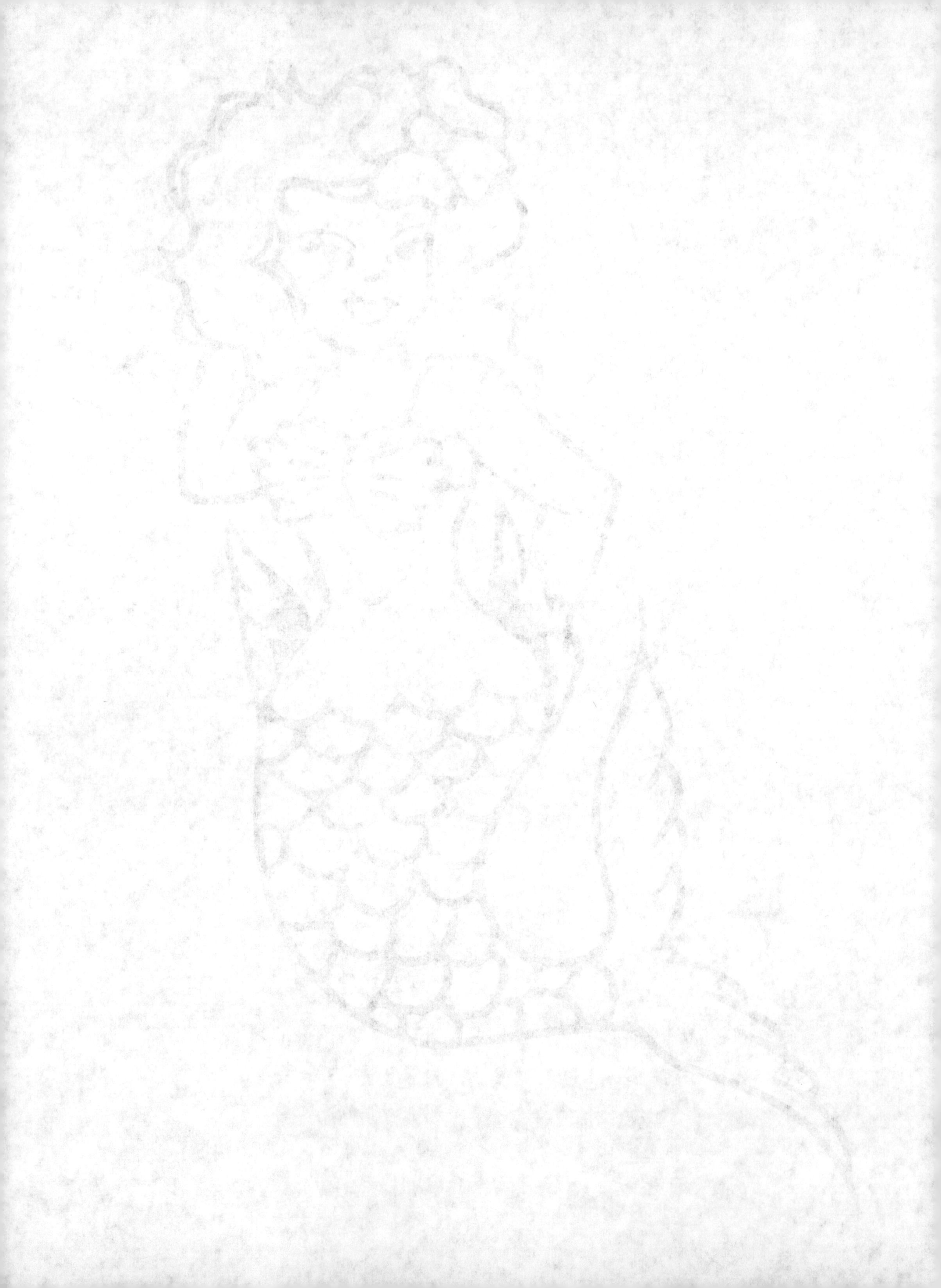

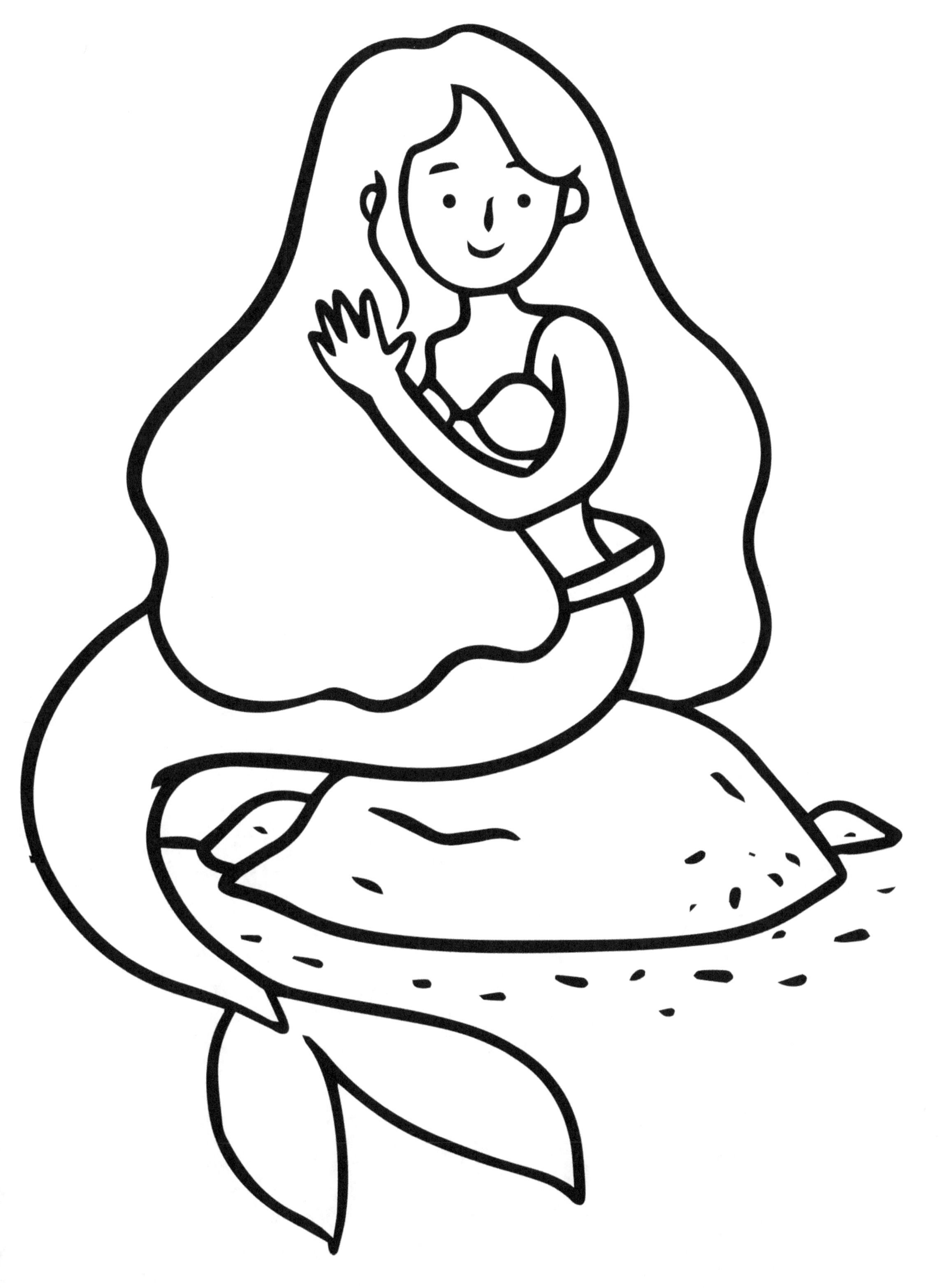

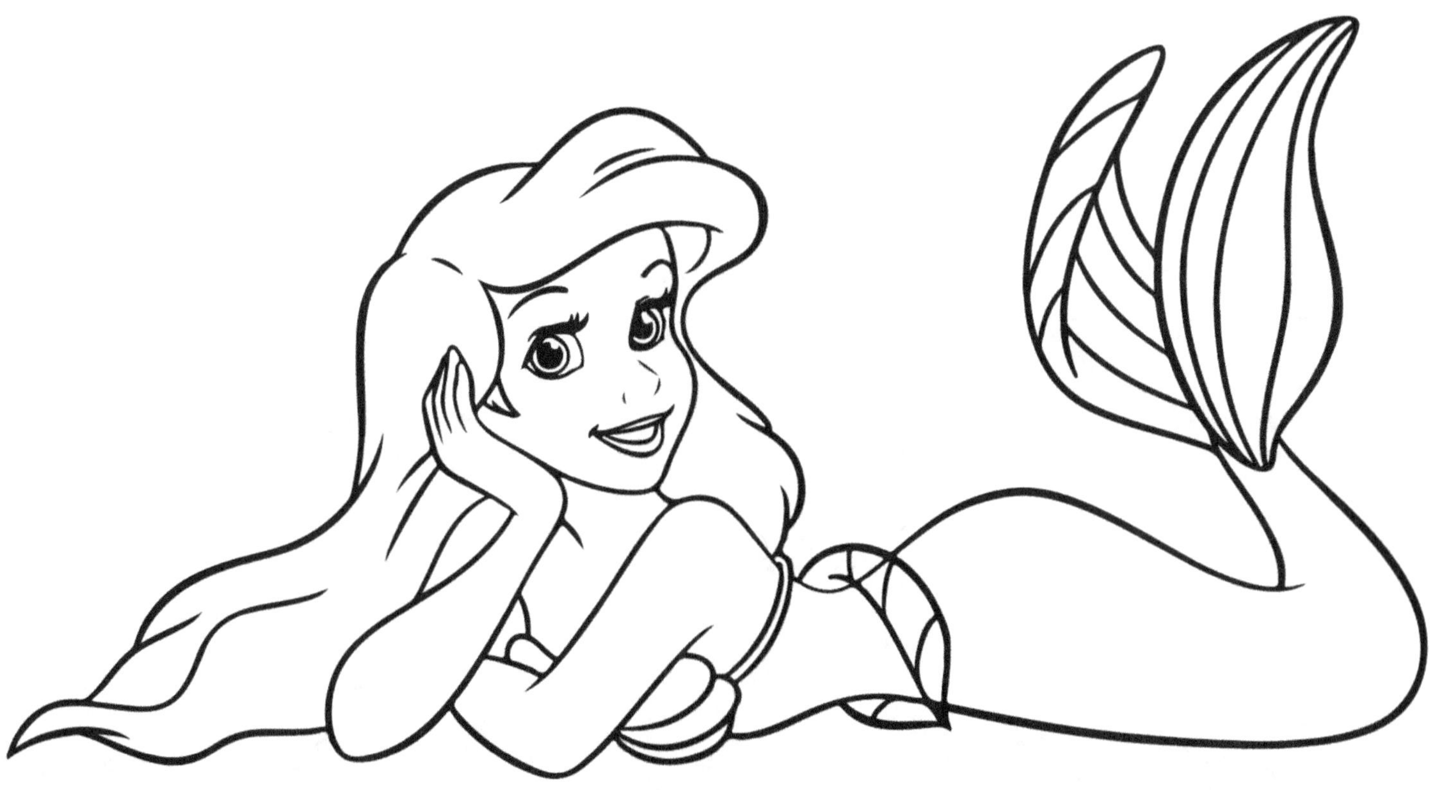

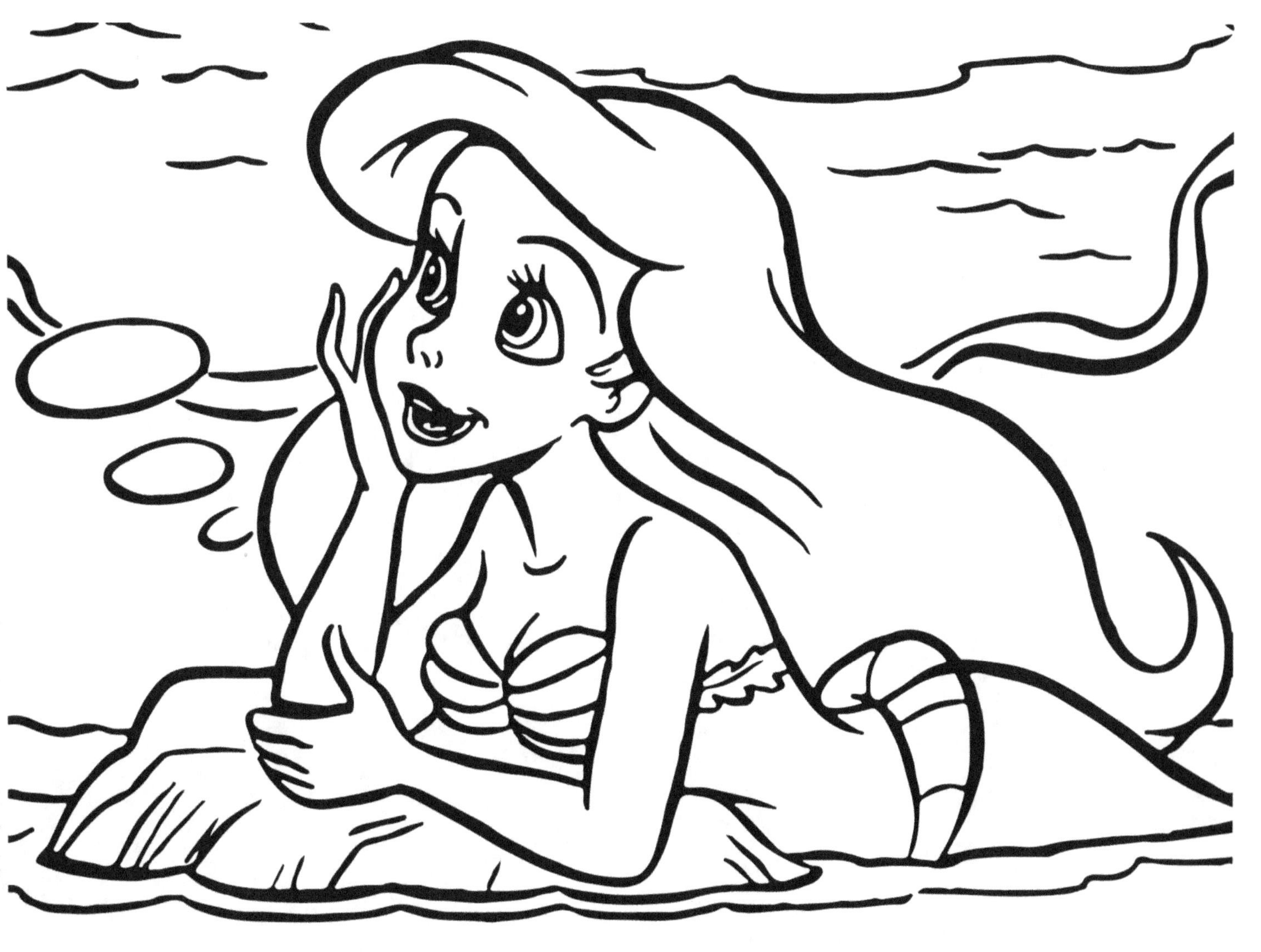

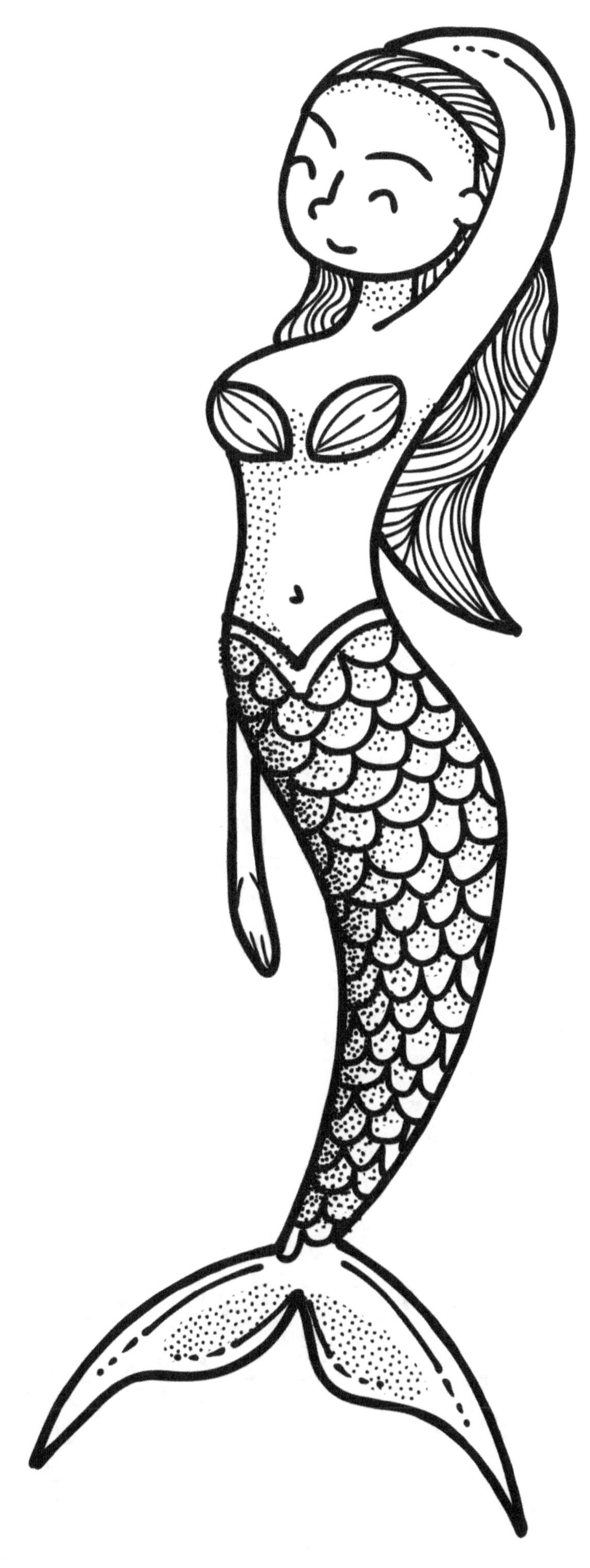

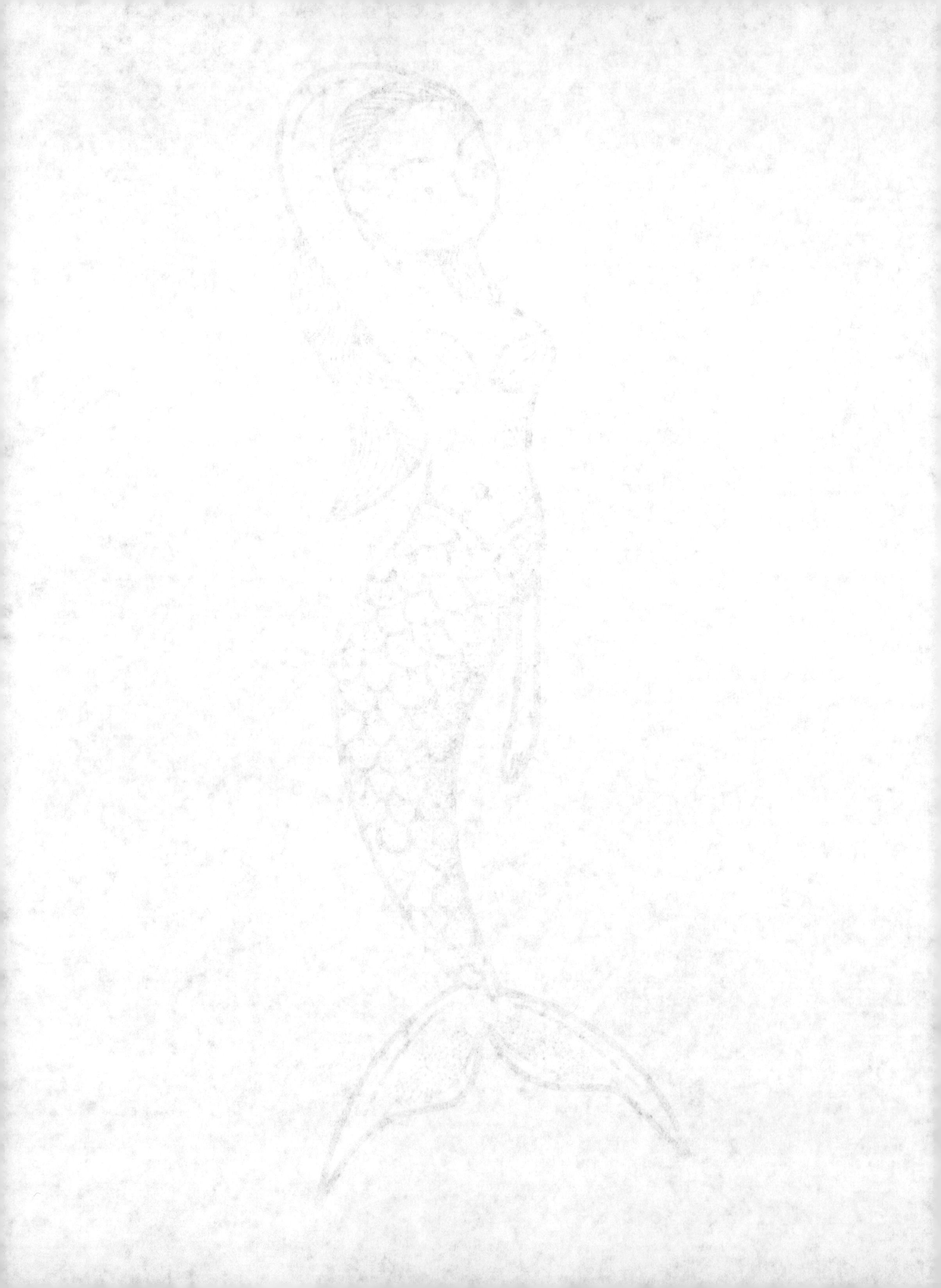

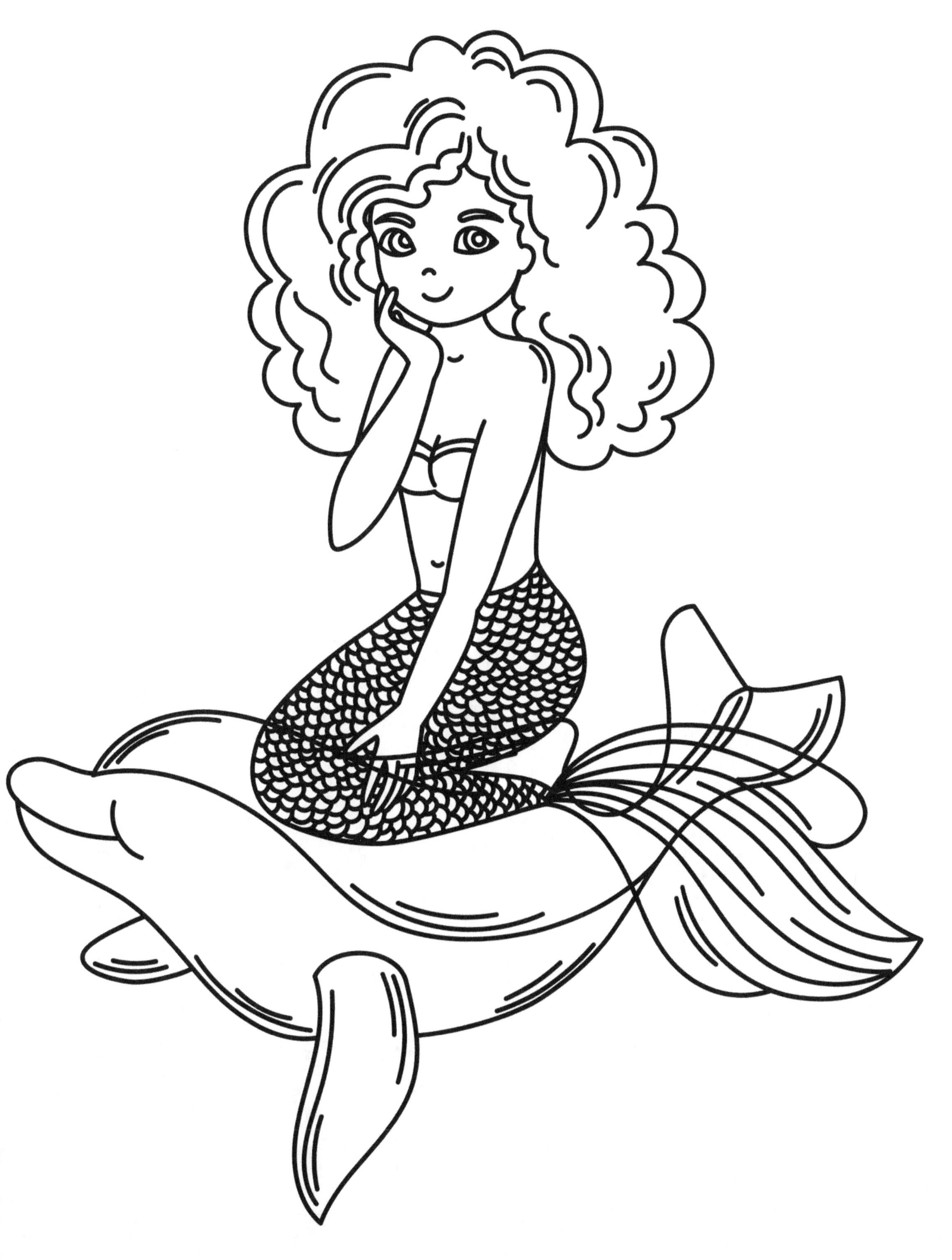

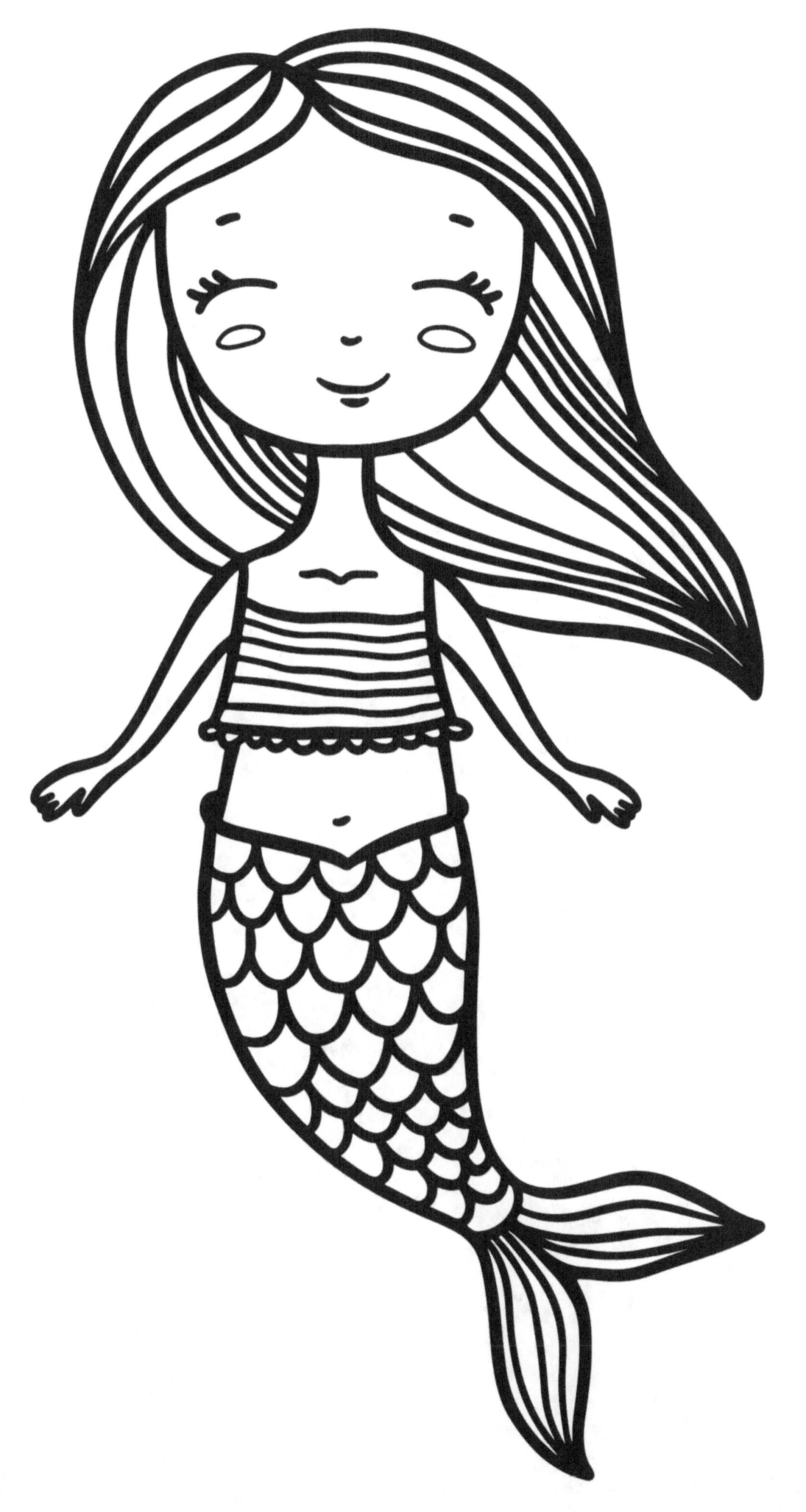

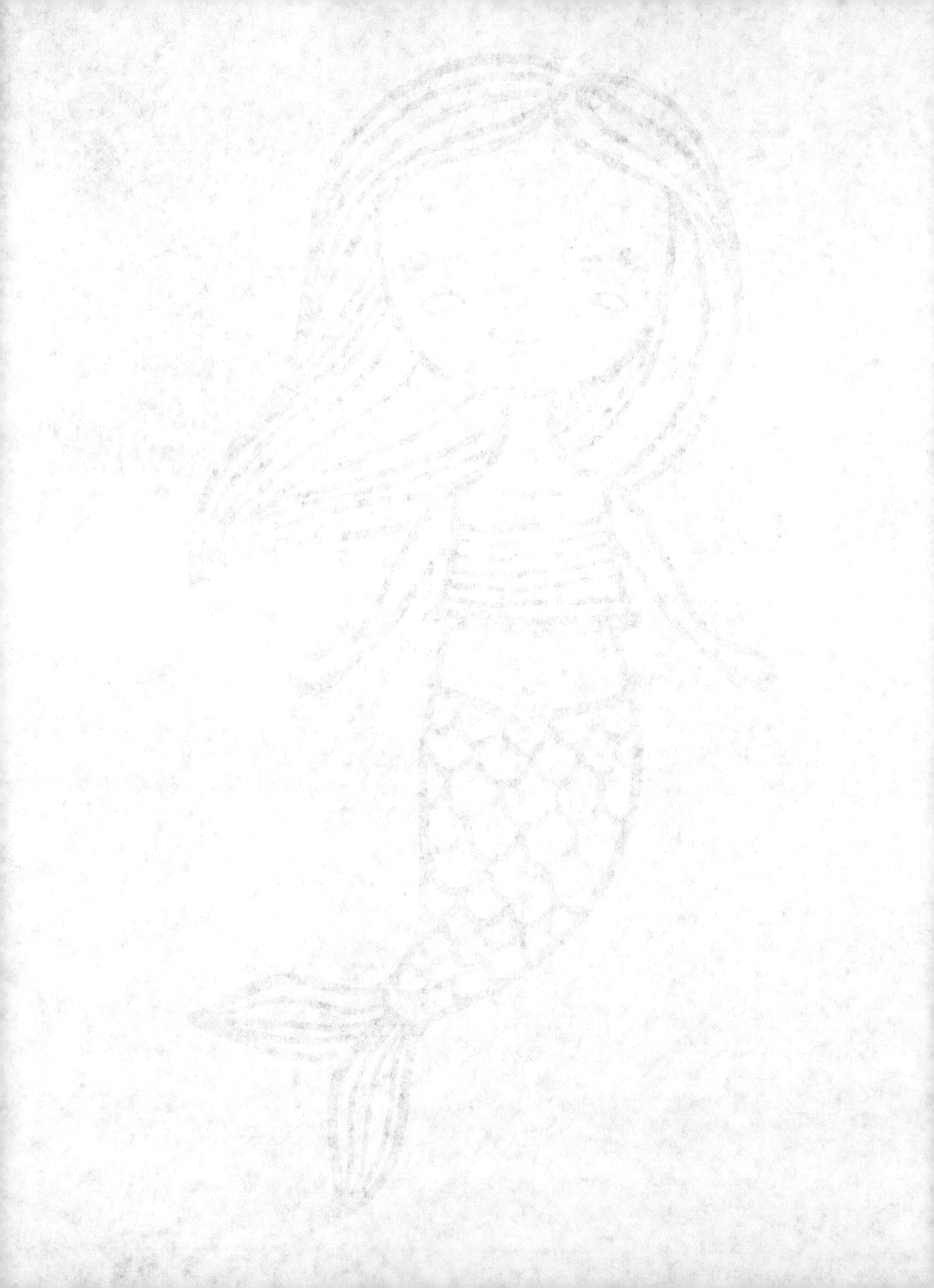

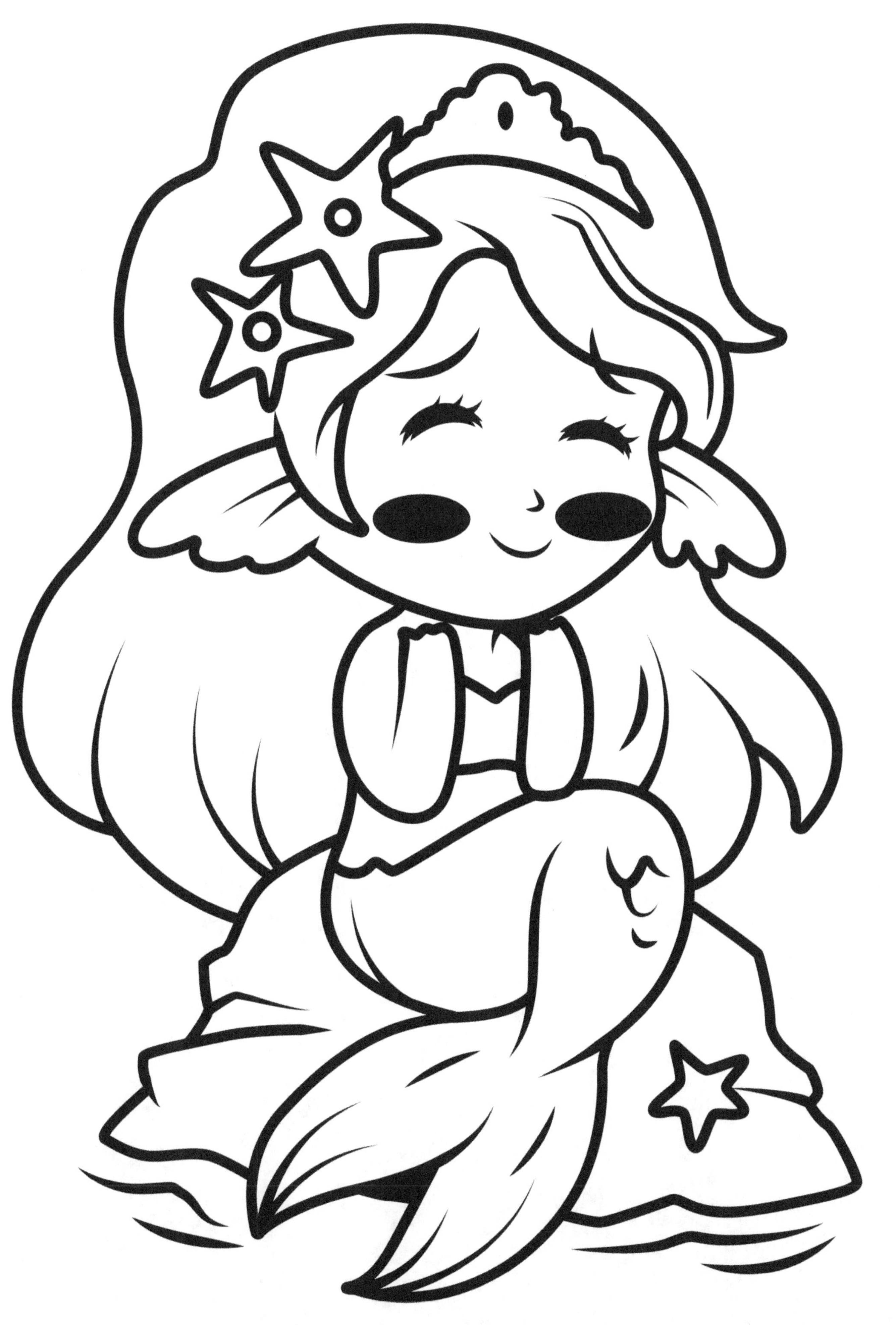

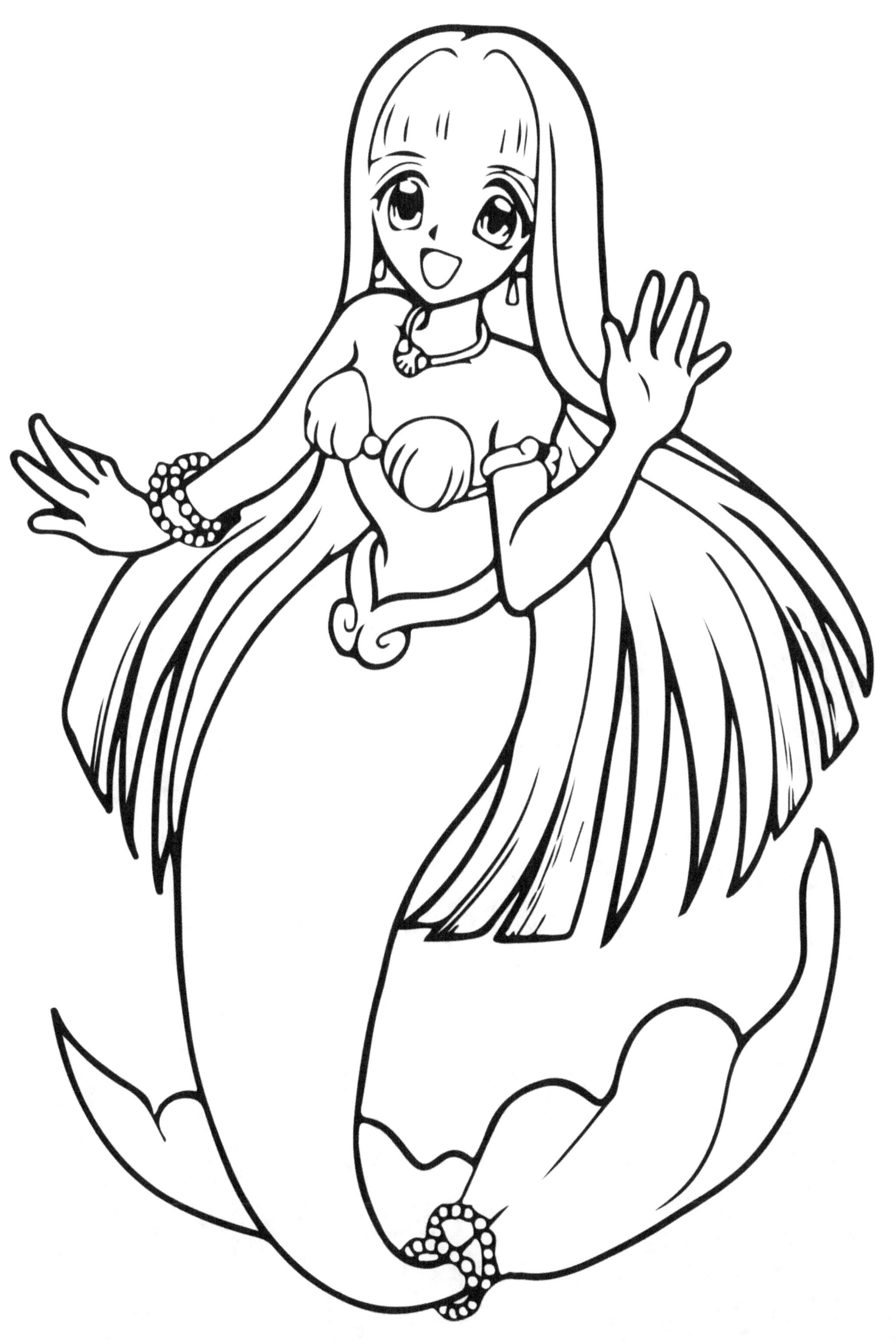

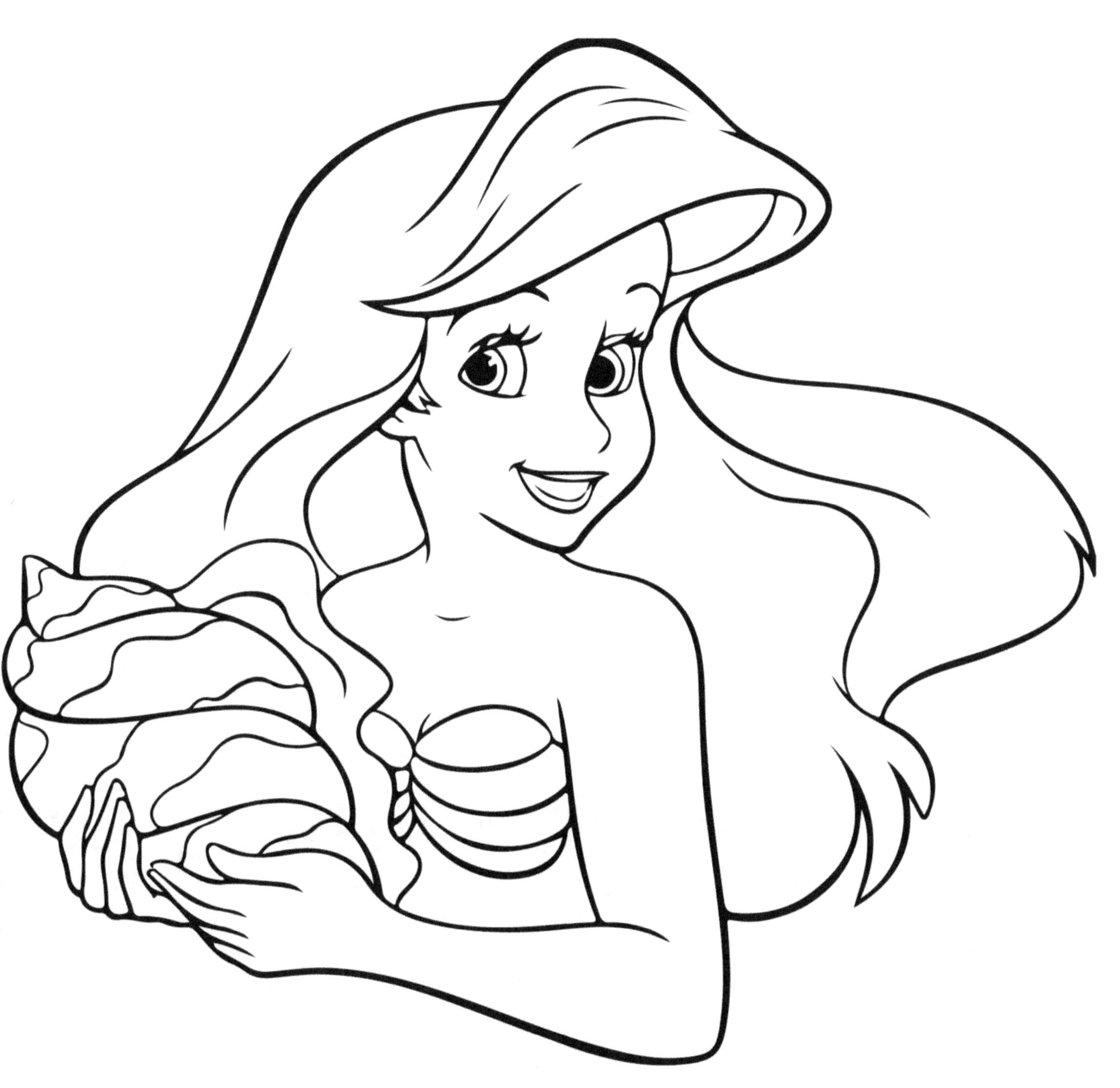

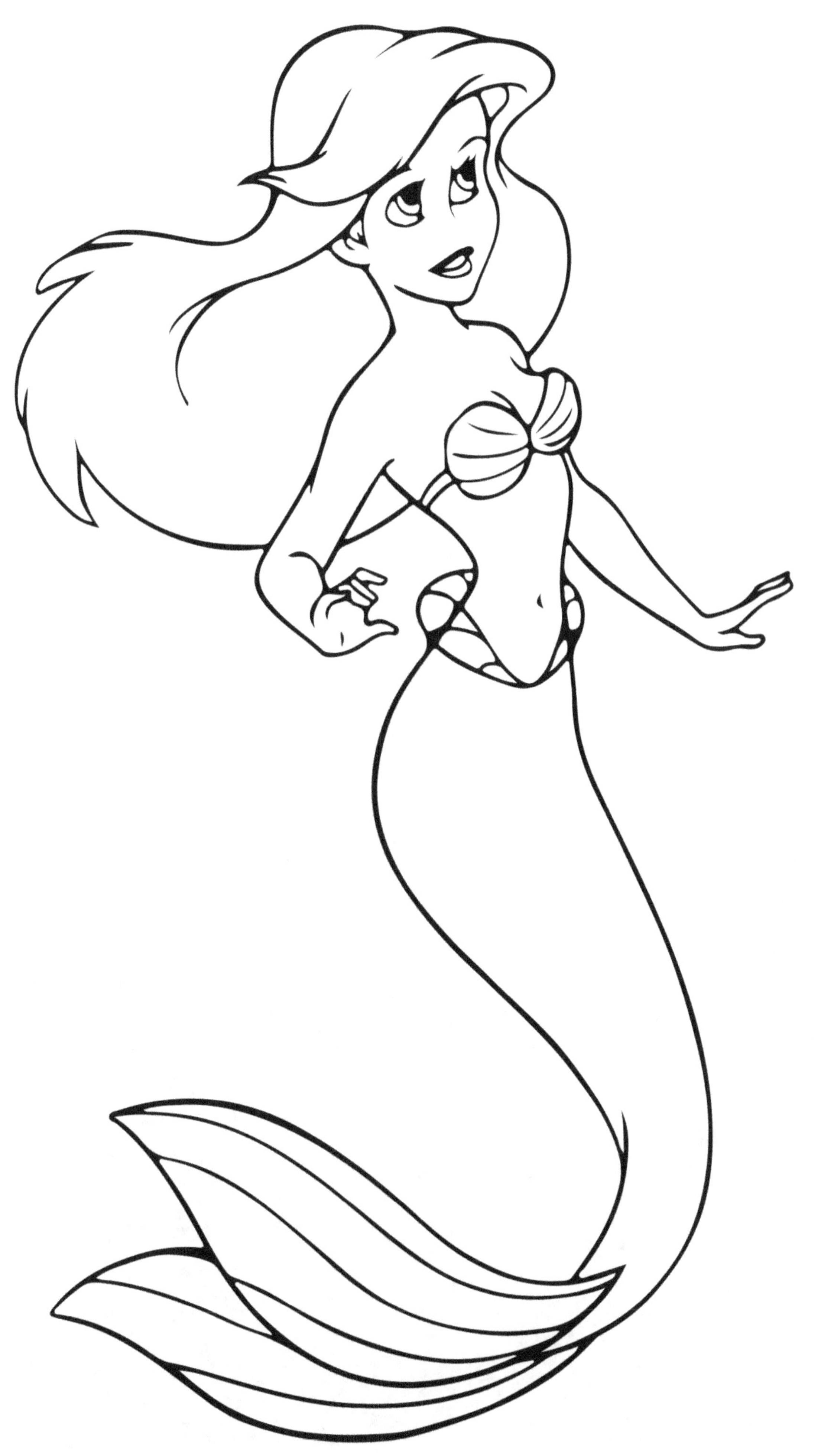

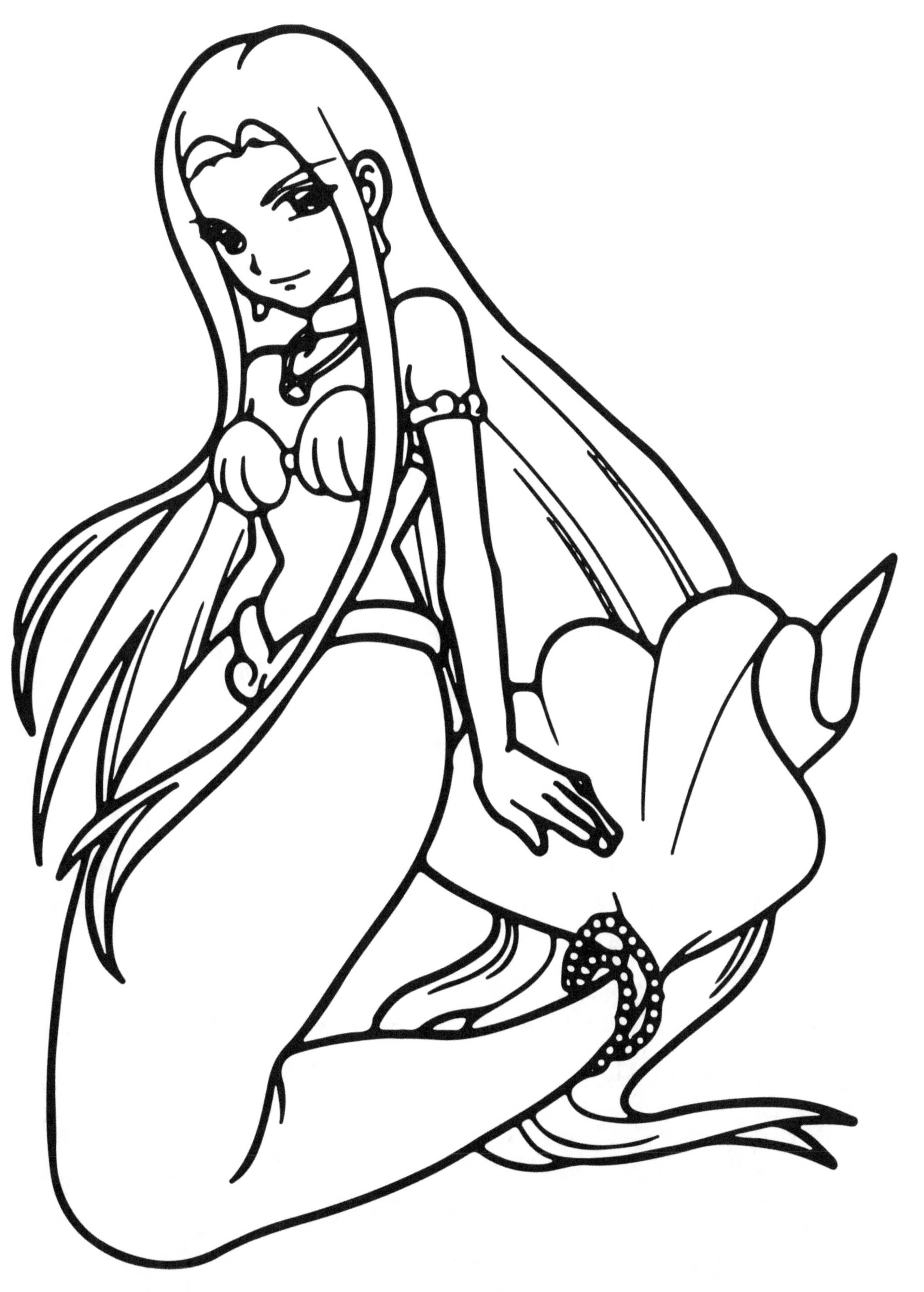

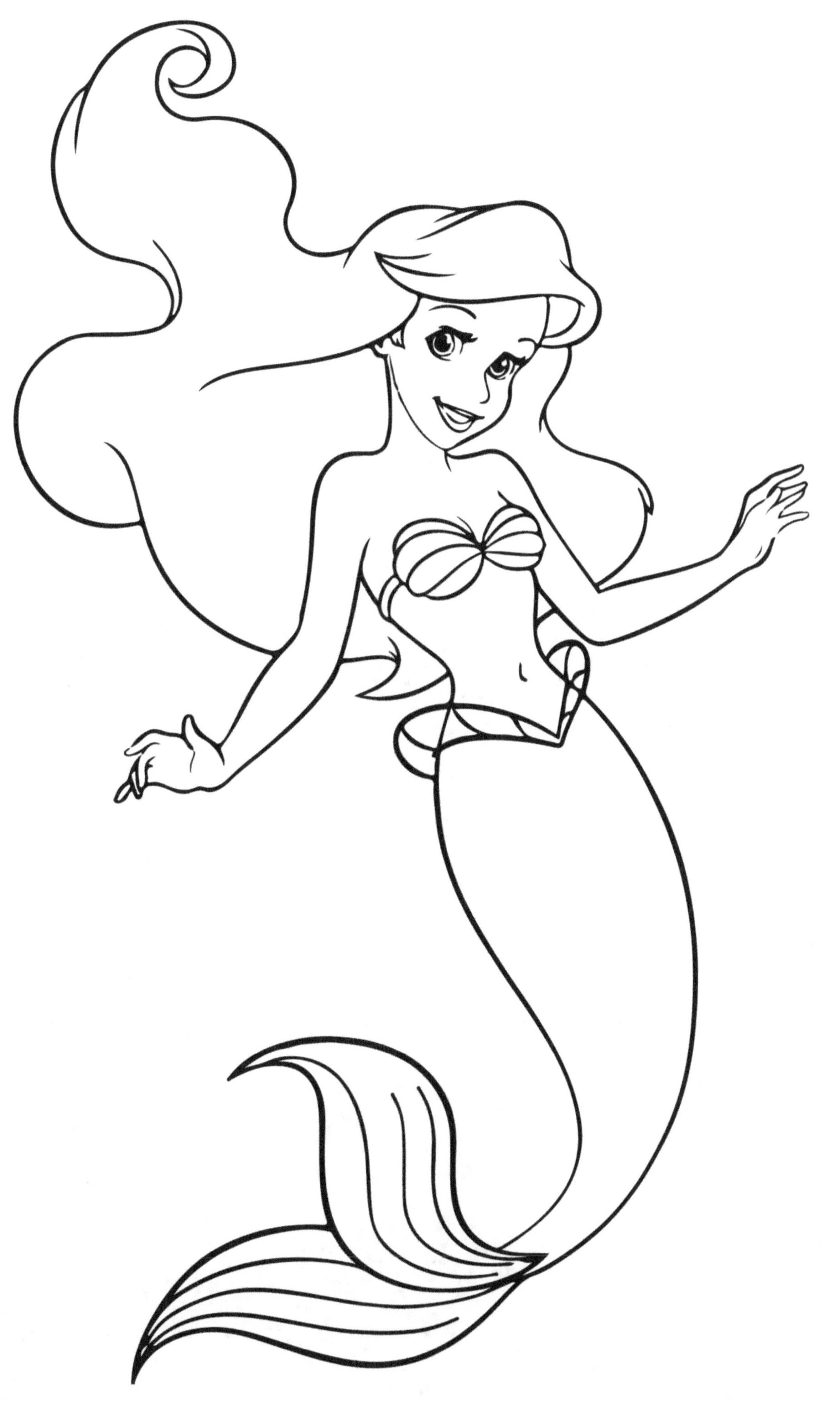

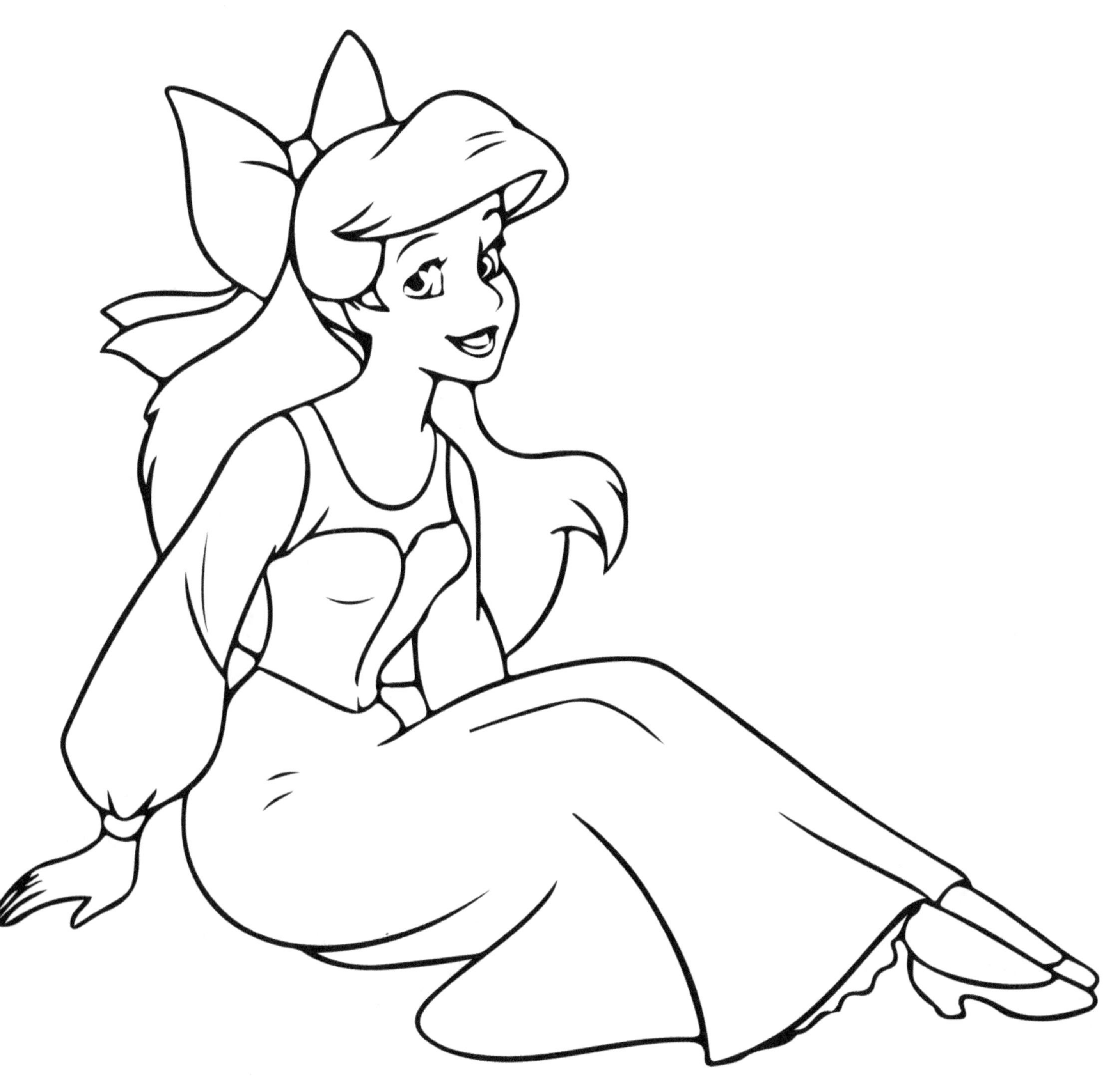

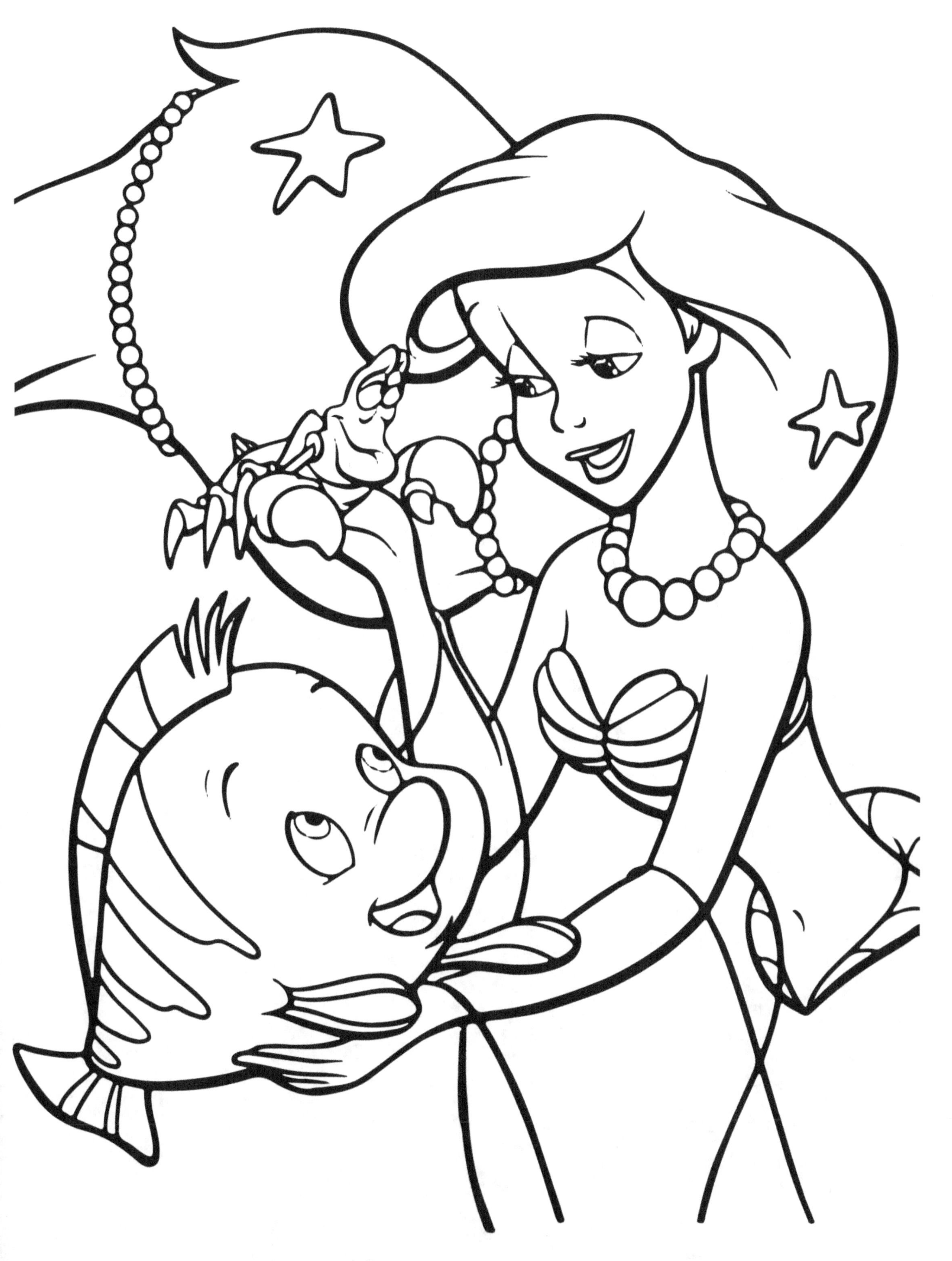

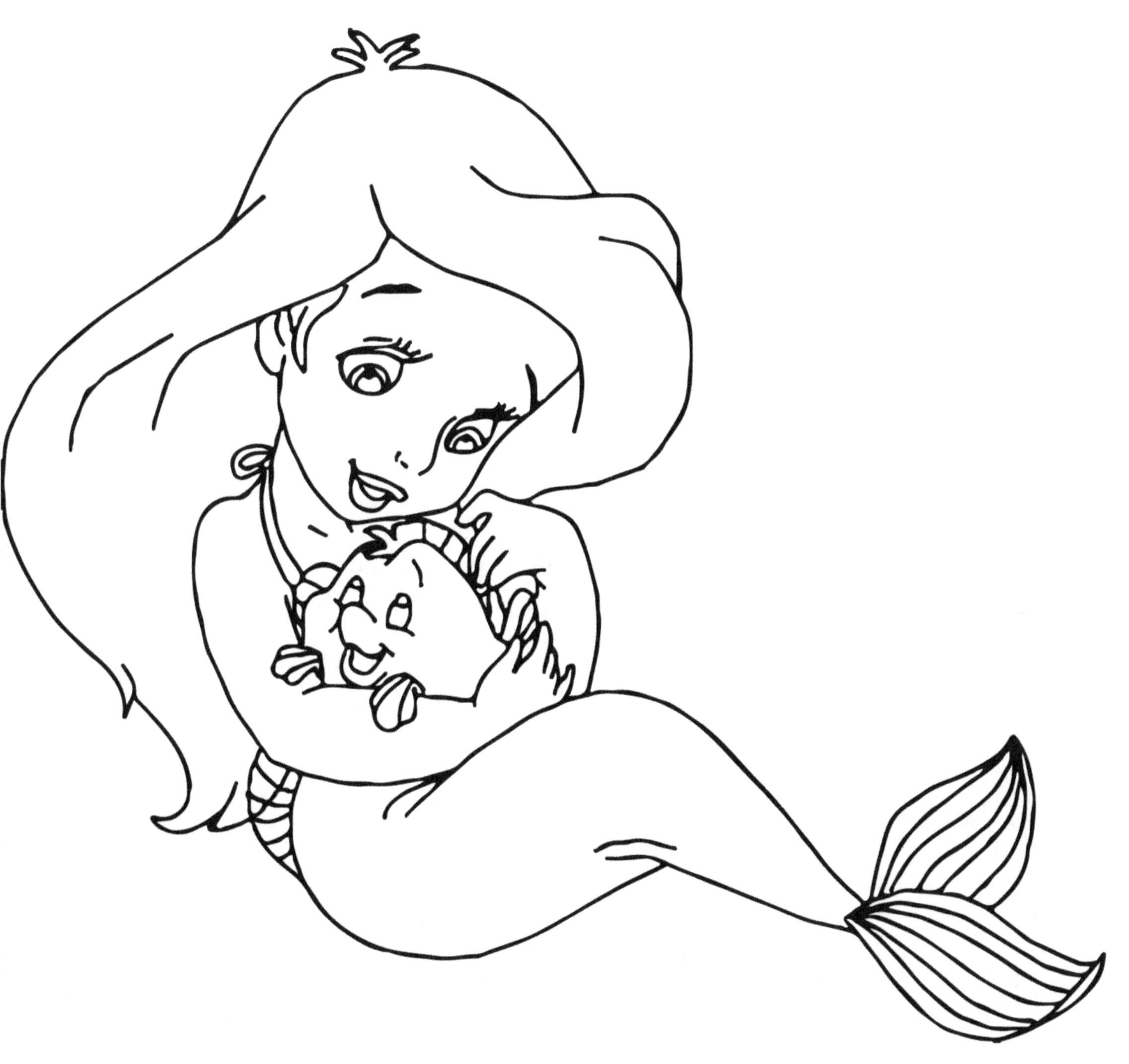

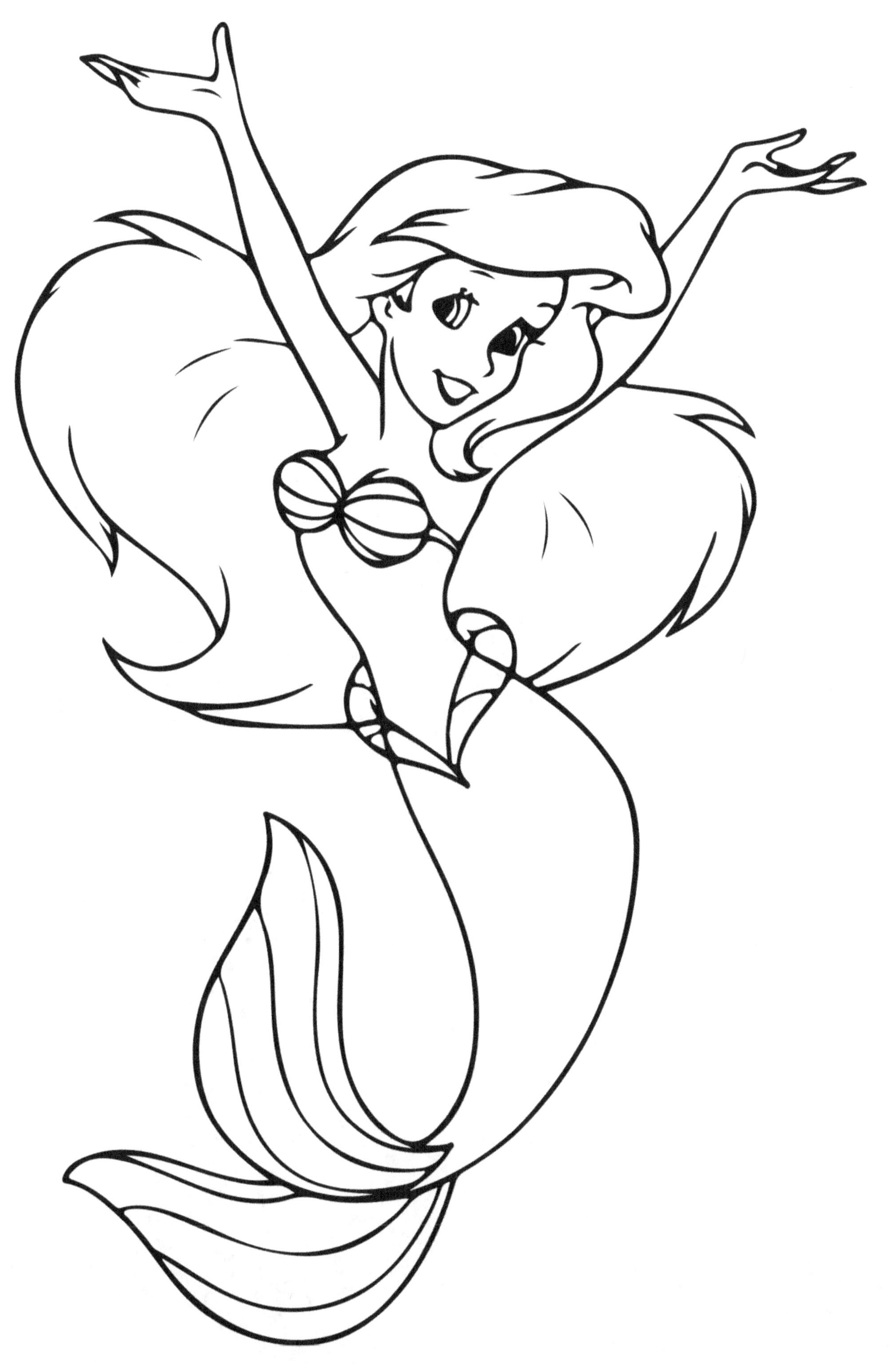

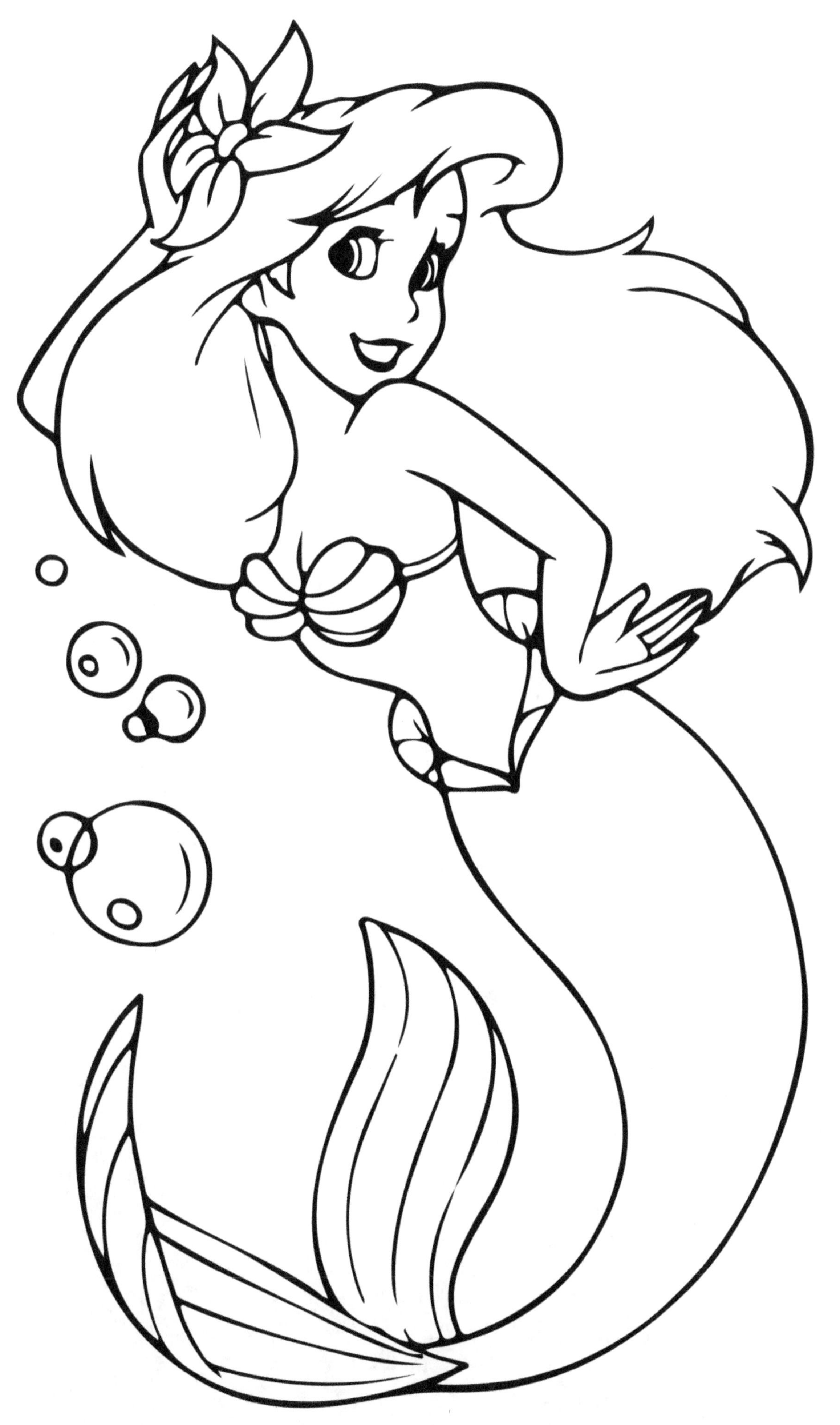

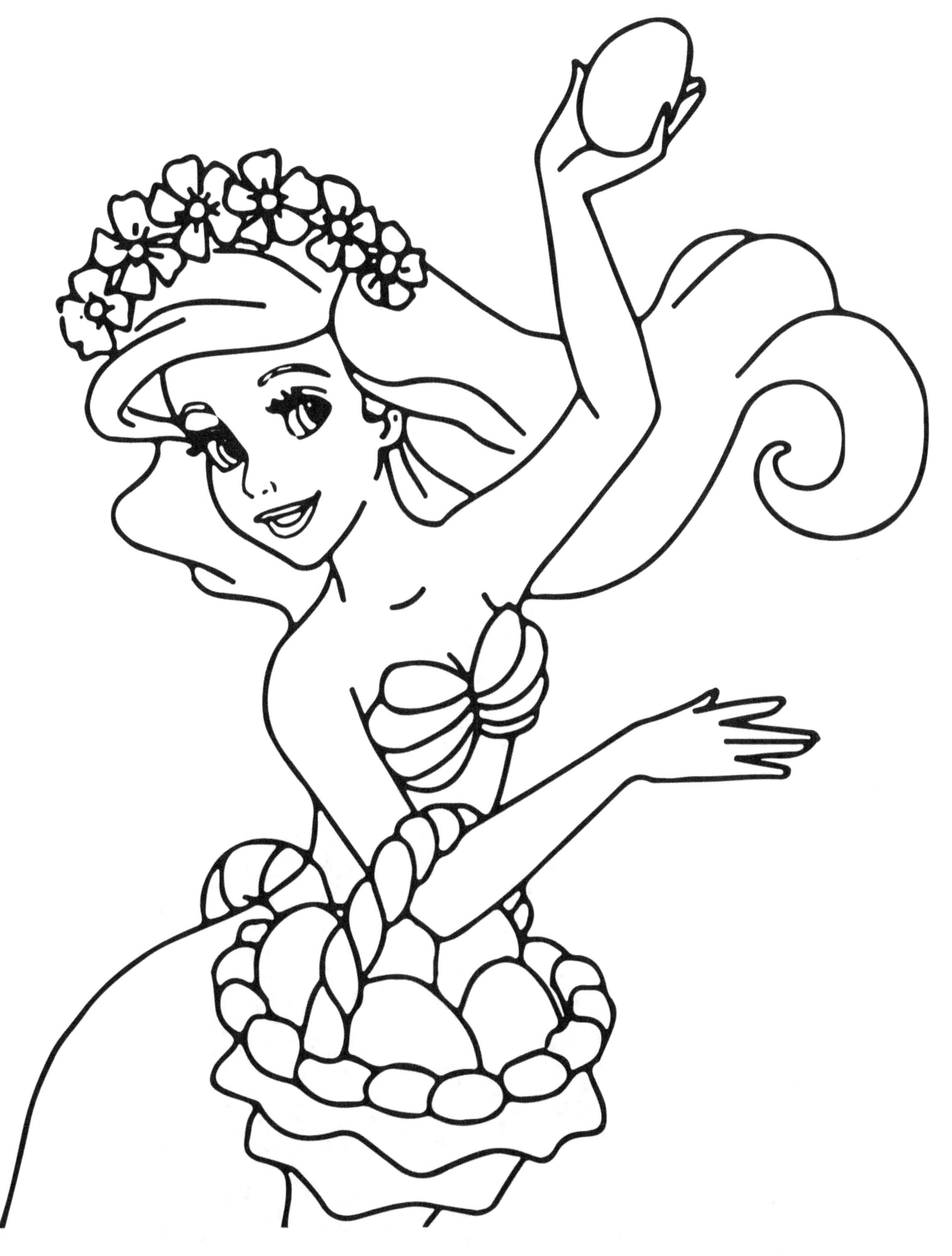

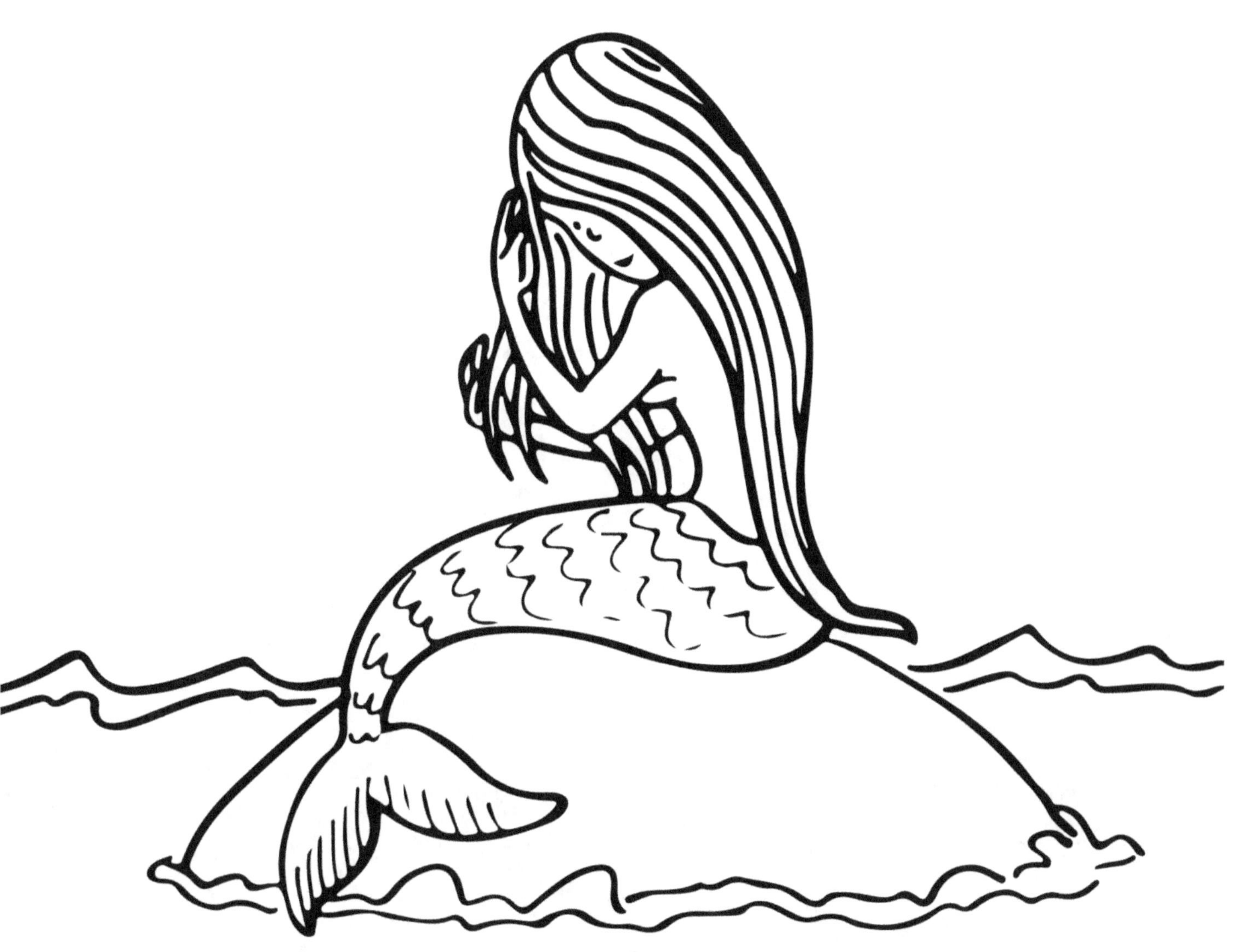

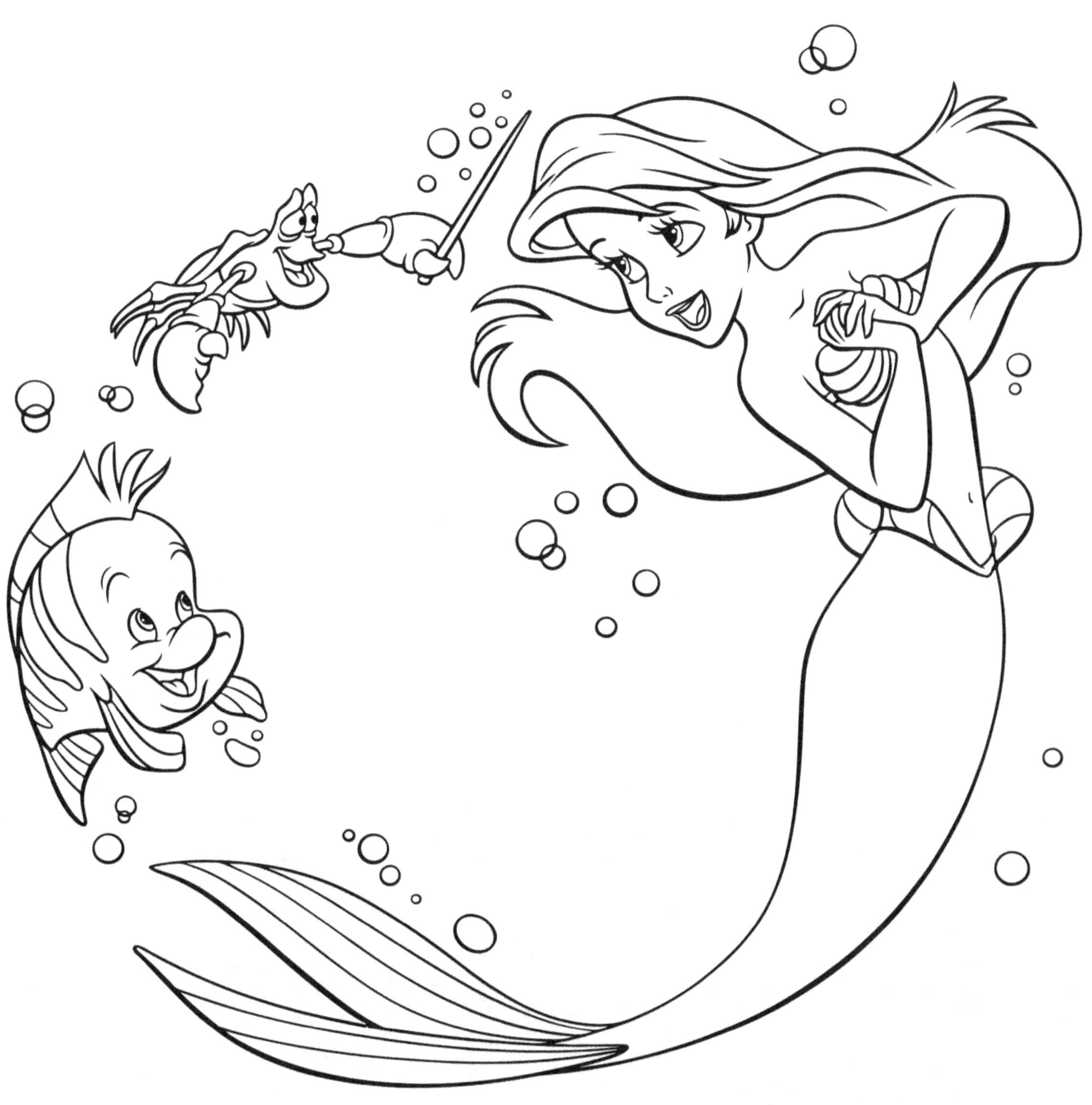

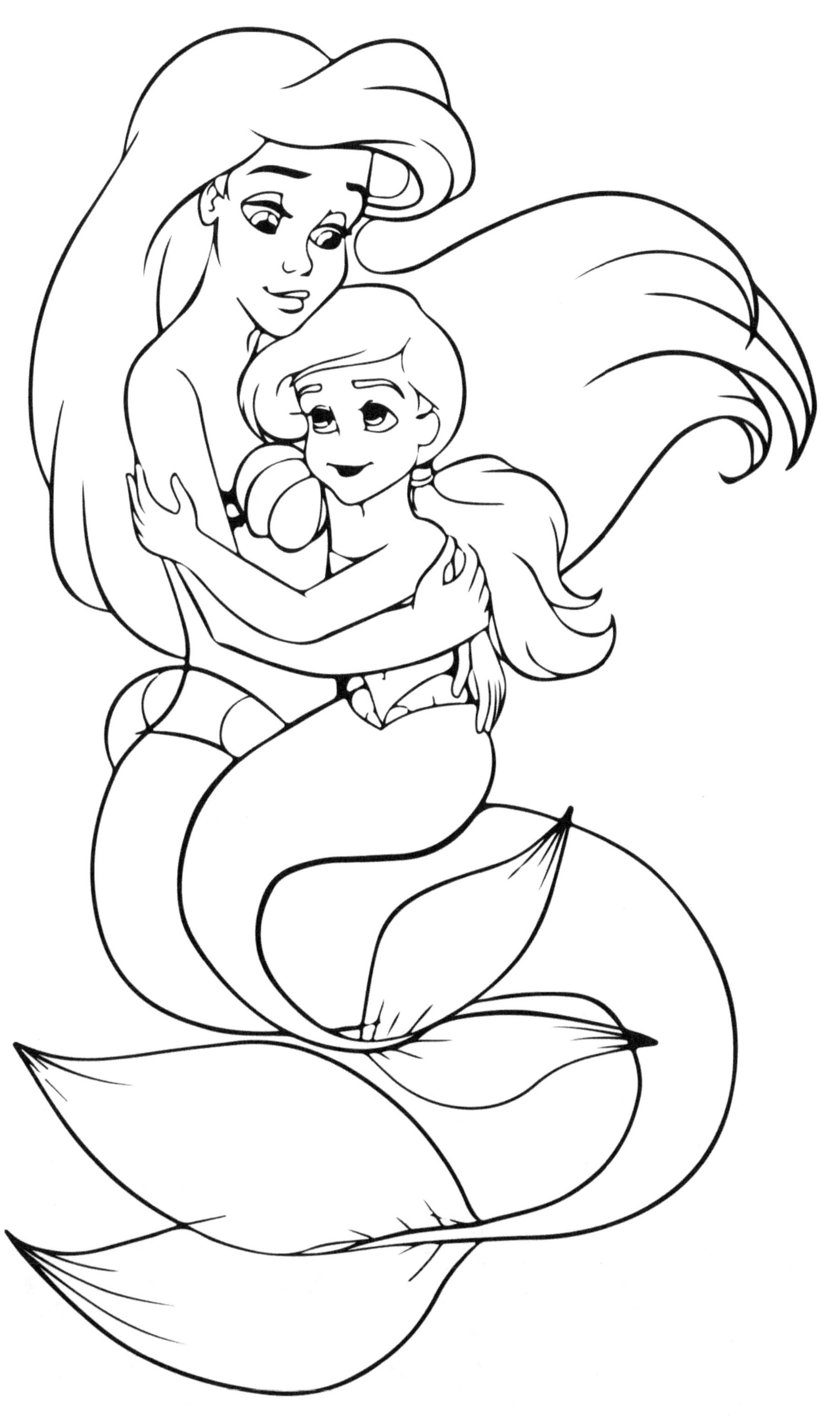